BRITISH AMERICAN
FOOTBALL
RULE BOOK

BRITISH AMERICAN FOOTBALL RULE BOOK

Edited by RADCLIFFE R. PHILLIPS

COLUMBUS BOOKS
LONDON

Copyright © 1987 Radcliffe R. Phillips

First published in Great Britain in 1987 by
Columbus Books Limited
19-23 Ludgate Hill, London EC4M 7PD

Printed and bound by
The Guernsey Press, Guernsey, CI

ISBN 0 86287 329 0

Contents

*This book is dedicated to my one true
tower of strength in difficult times,
Dee John - thanks a million.*

Foreword

The rules in this book are based on the rules of the NATIONAL COLLEGIATE ATHLETIC ASSOCIATION in America. These are the rules on which *all* other American rules are based. This rule book contains the basic rules of American Football. There exists a parallel publication of approved rulings and interpretations without which the game would be a boring succession of flags. The additional publication is used by the officials to ensure the game of football is played within the spirit and intent of the rules.

Radcliffe R. Phillips

Editor

The Football Code

The British American Football Code of Ethics states:
a. The football code shall be an integral part of this code of ethics and should be carefully read and observed.
b. To gain an advantage by circumvention or disregard for the rules brands a coach or player as unfit to be associated with football.

Football is and should be an aggressive, rugged, contact sport. However, there is no place in the game for unfair tactics, unsportsmanlike conduct or maneuvers deliberately designed to inflict injury.

Through the years the rules committees has endeavored by rule and appropriate penalty to prohibit all forms of unnecessary roughness, unfair tactics and unsportsmanlike conduct. But rules alone cannot accomplish this end. Only the continued best efforts of coaches, players, officials and all friends of the game can preserve the high ethical standards that the public has a right to expect. Therefore, as a guide to players, coaches, officials and others responsible for the welfare of the game, the committee publishes the following code:

Coaching Ethics

Deliberately teaching players to violate the rules is indefensible. The coaching of intentional holding, beating the ball, illegal shifting, feigning injury, interference or illegal forward passing, such as the "forward fumble," will break down rather than aid in the building of the character of players. Teaching or condoning intentional "roughing," including the blind side blocking of an opponent below the waist anywhere on the field, is indefensible. Such instruction is not only unfair to one's opponents but is demoralizing to the boys entrusted to a coach's care. It has no place in a game that is an essential part of an educational program. Changing numbers during the game to deceive opponents is an unethical act.

The football helmet is for the protection of the player and is not to be used as a weapon.
a. The helmet shall not be used as the brunt of the contact in the teaching of blocking and tackling.
b. Self-propelled mechanical apparatus shall not be used in the teaching of blocking and tackling.
c. Greater emphasis by players, coaches and officials should be placed on eliminating spearing.

The use of nontherapeutic drugs in the game of football is not in keeping with the aims and purposes of amateur athletics and is prohibited.

Illegal Use of Hand or Arm

Indiscriminate use of hand or arm is unfair play, eliminates skill and does not belong in the game. The object of the game is to advance the ball by strategy, skill and speed without using illegal tactics.

Perhaps a good game could be invented, the object of which would be to advance the ball as far as possible with the assistance of holding, but it would not be football. It would probably become a team wrestling match of some kind.

"Beating the Ball"

"Beating the ball" by an unfair use of a starting signal is nothing less than deliberately stealing an advantage from the opponents. An honest starting signal is good football; but a signal that has for its purpose starting the team a fraction of a second before the ball is put in play, in the hope that it will not be detected by the officials, is nothing short of crookedness. It is the same as if a sprinter in a 100-yard dash had a secret arrangement with the starter to give him a tenth of a second warning before he fired the pistol.

Illegal Shifting

An honest shift is good football, but shaving the one-second pause, shifting in such manner as to simulate the start of a play or employing any other unfair tactic for the purpose of drawing one's opponents offside can be construed only as a deliberate attempt to gain an unmerited advantage. Such tactics cannot be tolerated in football.

Feigning Injuries

An injured player must be given full protection under the rules. However, the feigning of an injury by an uninjured player for the purpose of gaining additional, undeserved time for his team is dishonest, unsportsmanlike and contrary to the spirit of the rules. Such tactics cannot be tolerated among sportsmen of integrity.

Talking to Your Opponents

Talking to opponents, if it falls short of being abusive or insulting, is not prohibited by the rules, but no good sportsman is ever guilty of cheap talk to his opponents.

Talking to Officials

When an official imposes a penalty or makes a decision, he is simply doing his duty as he sees it. He is on the field to uphold the integrity of the game of football, and his decisions are final and conclusive and should be accepted by players and coaches.

a. On- and off-the-record criticism of officials to players or to the public shall be considered unethical.

b. For a coach to address, or permit anyone on his bench to address, uncomplimentary remarks to any official during the progress of a game, or to indulge in conduct that might incite players or spectators against the officials, is a violation of the rules of the game and must likewise be considered conduct unworthy of a member of the coaching profession.

Sportsmanship

The football player who intentionally violates a rule is guilty of unfair play and unsportsmanlike conduct, and whether or not he escapes being penalized he brings discredit to the good name of the game, which it is his duty as a player to uphold.

THE RULES

Diagram of Field

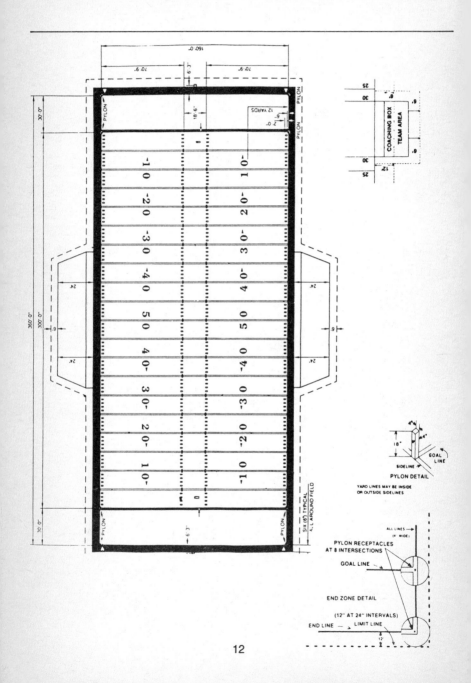

RULE 1

The Game, Field, Players and Equipment

SECTION 1. General Provisions

The Game
ARTICLE 1. a. The game shall be played between two teams of no more than 11 players each, on a rectangular field and with an inflated ball having the shape of a prolate spheroid.
b. A team legally may play with fewer than 11 players but is penalized if the following requirements are not met:
1. At least five men are within five yards of the restraining line when receiving a free kick (6-1-2).
2. At the snap, at least seven men are on the offensive scrimmage line, with not less than five numbered 50-79. (2-21-2) (7-1-3-b-1). (*Exception:* 1-4-2-b.)

Goal Lines
ARTICLE 2. Goal lines, one for each team, shall be established at opposite ends of the field, and each team shall be allowed opportunities to advance the ball across the other team's goal line by running, passing or kicking it.

Winning Team and Final Score
ARTICLE 3. a. The teams shall be awarded points for scoring according to rule and, unless the game is forfeited, the team having the largest score at the end of the game, including extra periods, shall be the winning team.
b. The game is ended and the score is final when the referee so declares.
c. The score of a terminated-suspended game shall be the final score at the time of the suspension.

Supervision
ARTICLE 4. a. The game may be played under the supervision of either three, four, five, six or seven officials: a referee, an umpire, a linesman, a field judge, a back judge, a line judge and a side judge. The use of a back judge, side judge and line judge is optional.
b. The officials' jurisdiction begins with the scheduled coin toss at midfield and ends when the referee declares the score final.

13

Team Captains

ARTICLE 5. a. Each team shall designate to the referee one or more players as its field captain(s) and one player at a time shall speak for his team in all dealings with the officials. A field captain's first announced choice of any options offered his team shall be irrevocable.

b. Any player may request a team charged timeout.

Persons Subject to the Rules

ARTICLE 6. All players, substitutes, coaches, trainers, cheerleaders in uniform, band members in uniform, mascots in uniform and other persons affiliated with the teams are subject to the rules and shall be governed by the decisions of the officials. Affiliated persons are those authorized within the team area.

SECTION 2. The Field

Dimensions

ARTICLE 1. The field shall be a rectangular area with dimensions, lines, zones, goals and pylons as indicated and titled in the field diagram.

a. All field dimension lines shown must be marked four inches in width with a white nontoxic material that is not injurious to the eyes or skin. (*Exception:* Sidelines and end lines may exceed four inches in width).

b. Short yard-line extensions inside or outside the sidelines and at the in-bounds lines promote greater accuracy in progress and spotting of the ball and are recommended.

c. All inside yard lines shall be four inches from the sideline.

d. Contrasting decorative material is permissible in the end zones but it can be no closer than four feet to any lines. Contrasting decorative material is permissible outside the sidelines and end lines.

e. If markings in the end zones are white or similar in color to goal lines, they shall be no closer than four feet to the boundary lines or goal lines.

f. Contrasting decorative material is permissible within the sidelines and between the goal lines, but shall not obliterate yard lines, goal lines or sidelines.

g. Goal lines may be of contrasting colors.

h. Commercial advertising is prohibited on the field.

i. Field yard-line numbers measuring six feet in height and four feet in width nine yards from the in-bounds line are recommended.

Marking Boundary Areas

ARTICLE 2. Measurements shall be from the inside edges of the boundary markings. The area enclosed by the sidelines and end lines is "in bounds" and the area surrounding and including the sidelines and end lines is "out of bounds." The entire width of each goal line shall be in the end zone.

Limit Lines and Coaching Lines

ARTICLE 3. a. Limit lines shall be marked with 12-inch lines and at 24-inch intervals 12 feet outside the sidelines and the end lines, except in stadiums where total field surface does not permit. In these stadiums, the limit lines shall not be less than six feet from the sidelines and end lines. Limit lines shall be four inches in width and may be yellow. No person outside the team area shall be within the limit lines. (see Rules 9-1-5-a, 9-2-1-b-1 and field diagram).

b. It is recommended that the limit lines continue six feet from the team area around the side and back of the team area.

c. A coaching line shall be marked with a solid line six feet outside the sideline between the 30-yard lines.

d. A four-inch-by-four-inch mark at each five-yard line extended between the goal lines as an extension of the coaching line is recommended for yardage chain and down indicator six-foot reference points.

Team Area

ARTICLE 4. a. On each side of the field, a team area back of the limit line and between the 25- or 30-yard lines shall be marked for the exclusive use of substitutes, trainers and other persons affiliated with the team. The area between the coaching line and the limit line between the 30-yard lines shall either be white throughout, contain white diagonal lines or be marked distinctly for use of coaches.

b. The team area shall be limited to players in uniform and a maximum of 40 other individuals directly involved in the game. The 40 individuals not in uniform shall wear special identification.

c. Coaches are permitted in the area between the limit line and coaching line between the 30-yard lines. This area is the coaching box.

d. No media personnel, including journalists, radio and television personnel or their equipment, shall be in the team area or coaching box, and no media personnel may communicate in any way with persons in the team area or coaching box.

e. Game management shall remove all persons not authorized by rule.

Goals

ARTICLE 5. Each goal shall consist of two uprights extending at least 20 feet above the ground with a connecting white horizontal crossbar, the top of which is 10 feet above the ground.

a. Above the crossbar the uprights shall be white and 18'6" apart inside to inside.

b. The designated white posts and crossbar shall be free of decorative material. (*Exception:* 4-inch-by-42-inch orange wind directional streamers at the top of the uprights.)

c. The height of the crossbar shall be measured from the top of each end of the crossbar to the ground directly below.

d. "Offset uprights" may be used.

e. The following procedure is recommended when one or both goals have been taken down and the original goals are not available for a try or field goal attempt:

A team is entitled to a kicking try and is not required to attempt a two-point play if the goals are not in position or complying with the dimensions required by Rule 1-2-5. A team is also entitled to a field goal attempt under the same conditions.

Kicking tries and field goal attempts must be made in the direction of the goal the team was attacking when they elected to make the kick.

The home team is responsible for the availability of a portable goal if original goals are removed during the game for any reason. The portable goal shall be erected or held in place for the kicks.

Pylons
ARTICLE 6. Soft flexible four-sided pylons 4" x 4" with an overall height of 18 inches, which may include a two-inch space between the bottom of the pylon and the ground, are required. They shall be red or orange in color and placed at the inside corners of the eight intersections of the sidelines with the goal lines and end lines and at the intersections of the end lines and in-bounds lines extended.

Yardage Chain, Down Indicator
ARTICLE 7. The official yardage chain and down indicator shall be operated approximately six feet outside the sideline opposite the press box except in stadiums where the total playing enclosure does not permit.
a.   The chain shall join two rods not less than five feet high, the rods being exactly 10 yards apart when the chain is fully extended.
b.   The down indicator shall be mounted on a rod not less than five feet high.
c.   An unofficial auxiliary down indicator and an unofficial line-to-gain indicator may be used six feet outside the other sideline.
d.   Unofficial red or orange nonslip line-to-gain ground markers may be positioned off the sidelines on both sides of the field. Markers are rectangular, weighted material 10 inches by 32 inches. A triangle with altitude of five inches is attached to the rectangle at the end toward the sideline.
e.   All yardage chains and down indicator rods shall have flat ends.

Markers or Obstructions
ARTICLE 8. All markers and obstructions within the playing enclosure shall be placed or constructed in such a manner as to avoid any possible hazard to players. This includes anything dangerous to anyone at the limit lines. The referee shall order removed any markers or obstructions constituting such a hazard.

Field Surface
ARTICLE 9. No material or device may be used to improve the playing surface and give one player or team an advantage. (*Exception:* Rules 2-15-4 a, b.)

SECTION 3. The Ball

Specifications
ARTICLE 1. The ball shall meet the following specifications:
a.   New or nearly new. (A nearly new ball is a ball that has not been altered and retains the properties and qualities of a new ball.)
b.   Cover consisting of four panels of pebble-grained leather without corrugations other than seams.
c.   One set of eight equally-spaced lacings.
d.   Natural tan color.
e.   Two one-inch white stripes that are 3.00 inches to 3.25 inches from the end of the ball and located only on the two panels adjacent to the laces.
f.   Conforms to maximum and minimum dimensions and shape indicated in diagram.
g.   Inflated to the pressure of 12½ – 13½ pounds.
h.   Weight 14 to 15 ounces.
i.   The ball may not be altered.

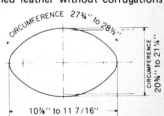

Diagram showing the longitudinal cross section of the standard ball. Maximum and minimum dimensions are used. This diagram is printed in order to secure uniformity in manufacture.

Administration and Enforcement

ARTICLE 2. a. The referee shall test and be sole judge of no more than six balls offered for play by each team prior to and during the game. The referee may approve additional balls if warranted by conditions.

b. Home management shall provide a pressure pump and measuring device.

c. The home team is responsible for providing legal balls and should notify the opponent of the type to be used.

d. During the entire game, either team may use a new or nearly new ball of its choice when it is in possession providing the ball meets the required specifications and has been measured and tested according to rule.

e. The visiting team is responsible for providing the legal balls it wishes to use while it is in possession if the balls provided by the home team are not acceptable.

f. All balls to be used must be presented to the referee for testing 60 minutes prior to the start of the game.

g. When the ball becomes dead nearer the sidelines than the hash marks, is unfit for play, is subject to measurement in a side zone or is inaccessible, a replacement ball shall be obtained from the ball person.

h. The referee or umpire shall determine the legality of each ball before it is put in play.

i. The following procedures shall be used when measuring a ball:
   1. All measurements shall be made after the ball is inflated to 13 pounds.
   2. The long circumference shall be measured around the ends of the ball but not over the laces.
   3. The long diameter shall be measured with calipers from end to end but not in the nose indentation.
   4. The short circumference shall be measured around the ball, over the valve, over the lace, but not over the cross lace.

SECTION 4. Players and Playing Equipment

Recommended Numbering

ARTICLE 1. It is strongly recommended that offensive players be numbered according to the following diagram that shows one of many offensive formations:

80-99	70-79	60-69	50-59	60-69	70-79	80-99
O	O	O	O	O	O	O
End	Tackle	Guard	Center	Guard	Tackle	End

O
Quarterback

O   O
Halfback   Halfback

Backs
1-49

O
Fullback

Mandatory Numbering
ARTICLE 2. a. All players shall be numbered 1 through 99.
b.   On a scrimmage down, at least five offensive players on the scrimmage line shall be numbered 50 through 79. (*Exception:* During a scrimmage kick formation, a player who initially is an exception to the 50-79 mandatory numbering in a scrimmage kick formation remains an ineligible receiver continuously during the down, and he must be positioned on the line of scrimmage and between the end players on the line of scrimmage.)
c.   No two players of the same team shall participate in the same down wearing identical numbers.
d.   Numbers shall not be changed during the game to deceive opponents.
e.   Markings in the vicinity of the numbers are not permitted.
PENALTY—5 yards from previous spot [S19].

Contrasting Colors
ARTICLE 3.a. Players of the opposing teams shall wear jerseys of contrasting colors; home teams have the choice of colors.
b.   Players of the same team shall:
    i.   wear jerseys of the same color
    ii. wear pants of the same color
    iii. wear helmets of the same color.

Mandatory Equipment
ARTICLE 4. All players shall wear the following mandatory equipment, which shall be professionally manufactured and not altered to decrease protection:
a.   Soft knee pads at least a half-inch thick worn over the knees and covered by pants.
b.   Head protectors with a secured four-point chin strap. If chin strap is not secured, it is a violation. Officials should inform players when less than four snaps are secured without charging a timeout unless the player ignores the warning.
c.   Shoulder pads, hip pads with tailbone protector, thigh guards.
d.   An intra-oral mouthpiece that covers all upper jaw teeth.
e.   A jersey with sleeves that completely cover the shoulder pads that is not altered or designed to tear and conforms with Rule 1-4-4-f.
f.   Permanent Arabic block or Gothic numerals on the jersey at least eight and 10 inches in height front and back, respectively, of a color in distinct contrast with the jersey, and each player shall have the same color numbers. A solid color border is permitted. The individual bars must be approximately one and one-half inches wide. Identical numbers shall be worn on front and back of each player's jersey.
g.   Sponsors name or advertising shall be contained in an area not exceeding 32 sq. inches in total. Sponsors logos or advertising may be worn on the sleeves but must be no more than 4 inches in diameter. Advertising must not be worn on the helmet.

NOTE: If a player is not wearing mandatory equipment in compliance in all respects with Rule 1-4-4, the team shall be charged a timeout. **VIOLATION — See Rule 3-3-6 and 3-4-2-b-2 [S23, S3 or S21].**

NOCSAE:* All players shall wear head protectors that carry the manufacturer's or reconditioner's certification indicating satisfaction of NOCSAE test standards. All such reconditioned helmets shall show recertification to indicate satisfaction with the NOCSAE test standard.

*National Operating Committee on Standards for Athletic Equipment (USA).

Illegal Equipment

ARTICLE 5. No player wearing illegal equipment shall be permitted to play. Any question as to the legality of a player's equipment shall be decided by the umpire. Illegal equipment includes:

a. Equipment worn by a player which, in the opinion of the umpire, would confuse his opponents or any equipment including artificial limbs that would endanger other players.

b. Hard, abrasive or unyielding substances on the hand, wrist, forearm or elbow of any player unless covered on all sides with closed-cell, slow-recovery foam padding no less than one-half inch thick or an alternate material of the same minimum thickness and similar physical properties. Hard or unyielding substances are permitted only to protect an injury and hand and arm protectors (casts or splints) are permitted only to protect a fracture or dislocation.

c. Hard or unyielding substances in thigh guards or shin guards unless such articles are covered on both sides and all of its edges overlapped with closed-cell, slow-recovery foam padding no less than one-half inch thick, or an alternate material of the same minimum thickness having similar physical properties. Therapeutic or preventive knee braces unless covered from direct external exposure.

d. Projection of metal or other hard substance from a player's person or clothing.

e. Shoe cleats — detachable:
   1. More than one-half inch in length (measured from tip of cleat to the shoe). (*Exception:* If attached to only one 5/32 inch or less high platform that is wider than the base of the cleat and molded to the sole.)
   2. Made of any material liable to chip or fracture;
   3. Without an effective locking device;
   4. With concave sides;
   5. Conical cleats with flat free ends not parallel with their bases or less than three-eighths inch in diameter or with rounded free ends having arcs greater than seven-sixteenths inch in diameter;
   6. Oblong cleats with free ends not parallel with bases or that measure less than one-quarter inch by three-quarters inch;
   7. Circular or ring cleats without rounded edges and a wall less than three-sixteenths inch thick;
   8. Steel tipped cleats without steel equivalent to SAE 1070 hardener and drawn to Rockwell C scale 42-45.

f. Shoe cleats — nondetachable:
   1. More than one-half inch in length (measured from tip of cleat to sole of shoe);
   2. Made of any material that burrs, chips or fractures;
   3. With abrasive surfaces;
   4. Made of any metallic material.

g. Tape or any bandage on a hand, wrist, forearm or elbow unless used to protect an injury and specifically sanctioned by the umpire.

h. Head protectors, jerseys or attachments that tend to conceal the ball by closely resembling it in color.

i. Adhesive material, grease or any other slippery substance applied on an attachment, a player's person or clothing that affects the ball or an opponent.

j.   Any face protector except those constructed of non-breakable material with rounded edges covered with resilient material designed to prevent chipping, burrs or an abrasiveness that would endanger players.
k.   Shoulder pads with the leading edge of the epaulet rounded with a radius more than one-half the thickness of the material used.
l.   Uniform attachments designating anything except player's numbers, player's name, school, game or memorial insignia. (This applies to towels or any other item attached to the uniform.)
m.   Gloves worn intentionally to closely resemble the opponent's jersey color or not in conformance with 1-4-5-b.

NOTE: No player wearing illegal equipment shall be permitted to play. If illegal equipment is discovered by an official, the team shall be charged a team timeout. **VIOLATION—See Rule 3-3-6 and 3-4-2-b-2 [S23, S3 or S21].**
   Exception: If equipment in Rule 1-4-5 becomes illegal through play, the player must leave the game but will not be charged a team timeout.

Mandatory and Illegal Equipment Enforcement
ARTICLE 6. Failure to wear mandatory equipment or the use of illegal equipment is enforced as follows:
a.   Each of the first three infractions for failure to wear mandatory equipment or wearing illegal equipment requires a charged timeout. The fourth infraction in a half requires a five-yard penalty. The delay for the fourth timeout could be the first violation for not wearing mandatory equipment or wearing illegal equipment. The first three timeouts could have been taken by the team as charged team timeouts.
   1. The timeouts are granted.
   2. There is no offset for the first three violations when an opponent has fouled.
   3. When timeouts are exhausted, the next violation is a dead-ball delay penalty at the succeeding spot.
   4. A timeout is called, the offending team is indicated by the referee and the captain and coaches are notified through the officials nearest the sidelines.
b.   Officials should ascertain before the ready-for-play signal if players are not wearing mandatory equipment or wearing illegal equipment. Only in an emergency should the 25-second clock be interrupted.
c.   No jersey may be changed on the field of play and such changes must be made in the team area of the player making the change. When it is determined that a jersey does not comply with 1-4-4-e and/or f, a team timeout will be charged to that team at the succeeding spot. If the team has expended its three timeouts, a delay will be charged under 3-4-2-b-2. Players may change torn jerseys during team timeouts and return to play. A player may change a jersey and return during a delay penalty only if the game is not further delayed by that action.
d.   Tape may not cover or partially cover a glove. Tape may be used to secure glove fasteners.

Coaches' Certification
ARTICLE 7. The head coach or his designated representative shall certify to the umpire prior to the game that all players:
a.   Have been informed what equipment is mandatory by rule and what constitutes illegal equipment.
b.   Have been provided the equipment mandated by rule.

c.   Have been instructed to wear and how to wear mandatory equipment during the game.
d.   Have been instructed to notify the coaching staff when equipment becomes illegal through play during the game.

Prohibited Signal Devices
ARTICLE 8. Players are prohibited from being equipped with any electronic, mechanical or other signal devices for the purpose of communicating with any source. (*Exception:* A medically prescribed hearing aid of the sound amplifier type for hard-of-hearing players.)

PENALTY — 15 yards and disqualification of the player. Penalize as dead-ball foul at succeeding spot [S27 and S47] .

Prohibited Field Equipment
ARTICLE 9. a. Television replay or monitor equipment is prohibited at the sidelines, pressbox or other locations adjacent to the playing field for coaching purposes during the game.
b.   Motion pictures or any type of film for coaching purposes are prohibited any time during the game or between the periods.
c.   Media communicating equipment, including cameras, sound devices and microphones, is prohibited on the field or in the team area or coaching box.
d.   Microphones may be used only on referees for penalty or other game announcements, if controlled by the referee, and may not be open at other times. Microphones on other officials are prohibited.
e.   Microphones attached to coaches for media transmission are prohibited during the game.

RULE 2

Definitions

SECTION 1. Approved Ruling and Officials' Signals

ARTICLE 1. a. An Approved Ruling (A.R.) is an official decision on a given statement of facts. It serves to illustrate the spirit and application of the rules. The relationship between the rules and an Approved Ruling is analogous to that between statutory law and a decision of the Supreme Court.

 If there is a conflict between the official rules and approved rulings and examples, the rules take precedence.

b. An official's signal [S] refers to the Official Football Signals 1 through 47.

SECTION 2. The Ball: Live, Dead, Loose

Live Ball
ARTICLE 1. A live ball is a ball in play. A pass, kick or fumble that has not yet touched the ground is a live ball in flight.

Dead Ball
ARTICLE 2. A dead ball is a ball not in play.

Loose Ball
ARTICLE 3. A loose ball is a live ball not in player possession during:
a. A running play.
b. A scrimmage or free kick before possession is gained, regained or the ball is dead by rule.
c. The interval after a legal forward pass is touched and before it becomes complete, incomplete or intercepted. *NOTE* — This interval is during a forward pass play and the ball may be batted in any direction.
d. All players are eligible to touch or recover a ball that is loose from a fumble or a backward pass, but eligibility to touch a ball loose from a kick is governed by kick rules (Rule 6).

When Ball is Ready for Play
ARTICLE 4. A dead ball is ready for play when the referee:
a.   If time is in, sounds his whistle and signals ready for play.
b.   If time is out, sounds his whistle and signals either "start the clock" or "ball ready for play."

In Possession
ARTICLE 5. "In possession" is an abbreviation meaning the holding or controlling of a live ball or a ball to be free kicked.
a.   A player is "in possession" when he is holding or controlling the ball.
b.   A team is "in possession" when one of its players is "in possession" or attempting a punt, drop kick or place kick, while a forward pass thrown by one of its players is in flight or was last in possession during a loose ball.

Belongs To
ARTICLE 6. "Belongs to" as contrasted with "in possession" denotes temporary custody of a dead ball. Legality of such custody is immaterial because the ball must next be put in play in accordance with rules governing the existing situation.

Catch, Interception, Recovery
ARTICLE 7. A catch is an act of establishing player possession of a live ball in flight.
a.   A catch of an opponent's fumble or pass is an interception.
b.   Securing player possession of a live ball after it strikes the ground is "recovering it."
c.   To catch, intercept or recover a ball, a player who jumps to make a catch, interception or recovery must have the ball in his possession when he first returns to the ground in bounds or is so held that the dead ball provisions of 4-1-3-a apply.
  1. If one foot first lands in bounds and the receiver has possession and control of the ball, it is a catch or interception even though a subsequent step or fall takes the receiver out of bounds.
  2. A catch by any kneeling or prone in-bounds player is a completion or interception (7-3-1 and 2) (7-3-6 and 7).

Simultaneous Catch or Recovery
ARTICLE 8. A simultaneous catch or recovery is a catch or recovery in which there is joint possession of a live ball by opposing players in bounds.

SECTION 3. Blocking

Legal Block
ARTICLE 1. Blocking is obstructing an opponent by legally contacting him with any part of the blocker's body.

Below Waist
ARTICLE 2. a. Blocking below the waist is legally making the initial contact below the waist with any part of the blocker's body against an opponent, other than the runner, who has one or both feet on the ground.
b.   Blocking below the waist applies to the original contact by the blocker. A blocker who makes contact above the waist and then slides down below the waist has not fouled. If the blocker first contacts the opposing player's hands, it is a legal "above the waist" block.

c. The position of the ball at the snap is the landmark that remains constant while Rule 9-1-2-e is in effect. Blocking toward the ball is always related to the position of the ball at the snap.

Chop Block
ARTICLE 3. A chop block is an illegal delayed block at the knee or below against an opponent who is in contact with a teammate of the blocker. A chop block is delayed if it occurs more than one second after a teammate contacts the opponent.

Frame (of the body)
ARTICLE 4. a. The frame of the blocker's body is the front of the body at the shoulders or below.
b. The frame of the opponent's body is at the shoulders or below other than the back (see Rule 9-3-3-a-1-c Exception).

SECTION 4. Clipping

ARTICLE 1. Clipping is an illegal block against an opponent occurring when the force of the initial contact, except against the runner, is from behind. This includes running or diving into the back, or throwing or dropping the body across the back of the leg or legs of an opponent other than the runner.
a. Position of the blocker's head or feet does not necessarily indicate the point of initial contact.
b. It is not clipping if a player turns his back to a potential blocker who has committed himself in intent and direction of movement.

SECTION 5. Crawling

ARTICLE 1. Crawling is an attempt by the runner to advance the ball after any part of his person, other than a hand or foot, has touched the ground (*Exception:* 4-1-3-b.)

SECTION 6. Down and Between Downs

ARTICLE 1. A down is a unit of the game that starts with a legal snap or legal free kick after the ball is ready for play and ends when the ball next becomes dead. Between downs is the interval during which the ball is dead.

SECTION 7. Fair Catch

Fair Catch
ARTICLE 1. a. A fair catch is a catch beyond the neutral zone by a player of Team B who has made a valid or valid illegal signal during a free kick or scrimmage kick that is untouched beyond the neutral zone.
b. A valid, invalid or illegal fair catch signal deprives the receiving team of the opportunity to advance the ball and the ball is declared dead at the spot of the catch or recovery or at the spot of the foul if the catch precedes the signal.
c. If the receiver shades his eyes from the sun, the ball is live and may be advanced.

Valid Signal
ARTICLE 2. A valid signal is a signal given by a player of Team B who has obviously signalled his intention by extending one hand only clearly above his head and waving the hand from side to side of the body more than once.

Illegal Signal
ARTICLE 3. a. An illegal signal is a valid or invalid signal by a player of Team B beyond the neutral zone when a scrimmage kick is made and a fair catch is not permissible by rule.

b. An illegal signal is a valid or invalid signal by a player of Team B when a free kick is made and a fair catch is not permissible by rule.

Invalid Signal
ARTICLE 4. An invalid signal is any signal by a player of Team B that does not meet the requirements of a valid signal.

SECTION 8. Forward, Beyond and Forward Progress

Forward, Beyond
ARTICLE 1. Forward, beyond or in advance of, as related to either team, denotes direction toward the opponent's end line. Converse terms are backward or behind.

Forward Progress
ARTICLE 2. Forward progress is a term indicating the end of advancement by the runner and applies to the position of the ball when it became dead.

SECTION 9. Foul and Violation

ARTICLE 1. A foul is a rule infraction for which a distance penalty is prescribed. A violation is a rule infraction for which no distance penalty is prescribed and that does not offset the penalty for a foul.

SECTION 10. Fumble, Muff, Touch, Bat

Fumble
ARTICLE 1. A fumble is loss of ball by a player in possession during his unsuccessful attempt to hold, hand, pass it backward or kick it.

Muff
ARTICLE 2. A muff is an unsuccessful attempt to catch or recover a ball that is touched in the attempt.

Batting
ARTICLE 3. Batting the ball is intentionally striking it or intentionally changing its direction with a hand or arm.

Touching
ARTICLE 4. Touching of a ball not in player possession denotes any contact with the ball. It may be intentional or unintentional and it always precedes possession and control. Touching of a loose ball by anyone or anything (other than a kick that scores a goal after touching goal posts) on a boundary line causes the ball to be out of bounds and dead at its most forward point in the field of play. (*Exception:* 6-1-4-a and b; 6-3-4-a and b.)

SECTION 11. Lines

Goal Lines
ARTICLE 1. Each goal line is a vertical plane separating an end zone from the field of play when a ball is touched or is in player possession. A team's goal line is that which it is defending.

Restraining Lines
ARTICLE 2. A restraining line is a vertical plane when a ball is touched or is in possession.

Yard Lines
ARTICLE 3. A yard line is any line in the field of play parallel to the end lines. A team's own yard lines, marked or unmarked, are numbered consecutively from its own goal line to the 50-yard line.

Inbounds Lines (Hash Marks)
ARTICLE 4. The two inbounds lines are 70'9" inbounds from the sidelines and divide the field of play into three.

SECTION 12. Handing the Ball

ARTICLE 1. a. Handing the ball is transferring player possession from one teammate to another without throwing, fumbling or kicking it.
b. Except when permitted by rule, handing the ball forward to a teammate is illegal.
c. Loss of possession by unsuccessful execution of attempted handing (muff by the recipient) is a fumble.

SECTION 13. Huddle

ARTICLE 1. A huddle is two or more offensive players grouped together after the ball is ready for play before or after they have assumed a scrimmage formation prior to the snap.

SECTION 14. Hurdling

ARTICLE 1. Hurdling is an attempt by a player to jump with one or both feet or knees foremost over an opponent who is still on his feet. "On his feet" means that no part of the opponent's body other than one or both feet is in contact with the ground.

SECTION 15. Kicks

Legal and Illegal Kicks
ARTICLE 1. Kicking the ball is intentionally striking the ball with the knee, lower leg or foot.
a. A legal kick is a punt, drop kick or place kick made according to the rules by a player of Team A before a change of team possession. Kicking the ball in any other manner is illegal.
b. Any free kick or scrimmage kick continues to be a kick until it is caught or recovered by a player or becomes dead.
c. A return kick is an illegal kick.

Punt
ARTICLE 2. A punt is a kick by a player who drops the ball and kicks it with his foot or leg before it strikes the ground.

Drop Kick
ARTICLE 3. A drop kick is a kick by a player who drops the ball and kicks it as it touches the ground.

Place Kick
ARTICLE 4. A field goal place kick is a kick by a player of the team in possession while the ball is controlled on the ground or tee by a teammate. If a tee is used, it may not elevate the ball's lowest point more than two inches above the ground.
b. A free kick place kick is a kick by a player of the team in possession while the ball is positioned on a tee or the ground or controlled by a teammate. If a tee is used, it may not elevate the ball's lowest point more than two inches above the ground.

Free Kick
ARTICLE 5. A free kick is a kick by a player of the team in possession made under restrictions that prohibit either team from advancing beyond or behind established restraining lines until the ball is kicked. A ball that falls from a tee and touches the ground may not be kicked.

Kickoff
ARTICLE 6. A kickoff is a free kick that starts each half and follows each try or field goal. It must be a place kick or a drop kick.

Scrimmage Kick
ARTICLE 7. A scrimmage kick is a kick by Team A during a scrimmage down before team possession changes. A scrimmage kick has crossed the neutral zone when it touches the ground, a player, an official or anything beyond the neutral zone.

Return Kick
ARTICLE 8. A return kick is a kick by a player of the team in possession after change of team possession during a down and is an illegal kick.

Field Goal Attempt
ARTICLE 9. A field goal attempt is any place kick or drop kick from scrimmage.

Scrimmage Kick Formation
ARTICLE 10. A scrimmage kick formation is a formation with at least one player seven yards or more behind the neutral zone and no player in position to receive a hand-to-hand snap from between the snapper's legs.

SECTION 16. Loss of a Down

ARTICLE 1. "Loss of a down" is an abbreviation meaning: "loss of the right to repeat a down."

SECTION 17. The Neutral Zone

ARTICLE 1. The neutral zone is the space between the two lines of scrimmage and is established when the ball is ready for play.

SECTION 18. Encroachment and Offside

Encroachment
ARTICLE 1. Encroachment occurs when an offensive player is in or beyond the neutral zone after the snapper touches the ball and prior to the snap or offensive players are not behind the restraining line when the ball is free kicked. (*Exception:* The snapper or the kicker and holder of a place kick for a free kick are not encroaching when they are beyond their scrimmage line or restraining line when the ball is put in play.)

Offside
ARTICLE 2. Offside occurs when a defensive player is in or beyond the neutral zone when the ball is snapped, illegally contacts an opponent beyond the neutral zone before the ball is snapped or is not within the restraining lines when the ball is free kicked.

SECTION 19. Passes

Passing
ARTICLE 1. Passing the ball is throwing it. A pass continues to be a pass until it is caught, intercepted by a player or the ball becomes dead.

Forward and Backward Pass
ARTICLE 2. a. An attempted backward pass is a live ball thrown toward or parallel to the passer's end line; an attempted forward pass is a live ball thrown toward the opponents' end line. During a forward or backward pass, the point where the ball first strikes the ground, a player, an official or anything beyond or behind the spot of the pass, determines whether it is a forward or backward pass.
b. When a Team A player is holding the ball to pass it forward toward the neutral zone, any intentional forward movement of his arm starts the forward pass. If a Team B player contacts the passer or ball after forward movement begins and the ball leaves the passer's hand, a forward pass is ruled regardless of where the ball strikes the ground or a player.

c. When in question, the ball is a pass and not a fumble during an attempted forward pass.

Crosses Neutral Zone
ARTICLE 3. a. A legal forward pass has crossed the neutral zone when it first strikes the ground, a player, an official or anything beyond the neutral zone. It has not crossed the neutral zone when it first strikes the ground, a player, an official or anything in or behind the neutral zone.
b. A passer has crossed the neutral zone when any part of his body is beyond the neutral zone.

Catchable Forward Pass
ARTICLE 4. A catchable forward pass is an untouched legal forward pass beyond the neutral zone and an eligible Team A player has a reasonable opportunity to catch the ball.

SECTION 20. Penalty

ARTICLE 1. A penalty is a yardage loss imposed by rule against a team that has committed a foul and may include a loss of down.

SECTION 21. Scrimmage

Scrimmage
ARTICLE 1. A scrimmage is the interplay of the two teams during a down in which play begins with a snap.

Scrimmage Line
ARTICLE 2. a. The scrimmage line for each team is the yard line and its vertical plane that passes through the point of the ball nearest its own goal line.
b. A player of Team A is "on his scrimmage line" at the snap when he faces his opponents' goal line with the line of his shoulders approximately parallel thereto and his head breaks the plane of the line drawn through the waistline of the snapper.

Backfield Line
ARTICLE 3. To be legally in the backfield, a Team A player's head must not break the plane of the line drawn through the rear-most part, other than the legs or feet, of the nearest Team A player (except the snapper) on the line of scrimmage.

SECTION 22. Shift

ARTICLE 1. A shift is a simultaneous change of position by two or more offensive players after the ball is ready for play for a scrimmage and before the next snap.

SECTION 23. Snapping the Ball

ARTICLE 1. a. Legally snapping the ball (a snap) is handing or passing it back from its position on the ground with a quick and continuous motion of the hand or hands, the ball actually leaving the hand or hands in this motion.

b. If, during any backward motion of a legal snap, the ball slips from the snapper's hand, it is a snap and in play, provided the ball had been declared "ready" (4-1-1).
c. While resting on the ground and prior to the snap, the long axis of the ball must be at right angles to the scrimmage line with neither end of the ball raised more than 45 degrees.
d. Unless moved in a backward direction, the movement of the ball does not start a legal snap. It is not a legal snap if the ball is first moved forward or lifted.
e. The snap need not be between the snapper's legs; but to be legal, it must be a quick and continuous backward motion.
f. The ball must be snapped on or between the in bounds lines.

SECTION 24. Spearing

ARTICLE 1. Spearing is the intentional use of the helmet in an attempt to punish an opponent.

SECTION 25. Spots

Enforcement Spot
ARTICLE 1. An enforcement spot is the point from which the penalty for a foul or violation is enforced.

Previous Spot
ARTICLE 2. The previous spot is the point from which the ball was last put in play.

Succeeding Spot
ARTICLE 3. The succeeding spot, as related to a foul, is the point at which the ball would next be put in play if that foul had not occurred. The try may not be the succeeding spot unless the ball has been declared ready for play on the try.

Dead-Ball Spot
ARTICLE 4. The dead-ball spot is the point at which the ball became dead.

Spot of the Foul
ARTICLE 5. The spot of the foul is the point at which that foul occurs. If out of bounds between the goal lines, it shall be the intersection of the nearer in-bounds line and the yard line extended through the spot of the foul.

Out-of-Bounds Spot
ARTICLE 6. The out-of-bounds spot is the point at which, according to the rule, the ball becomes dead because of going or being declared out of bounds.

In-Bounds Spot
ARTICLE 7. The in-bounds spot is the intersection of the nearer in-bounds line and the yard line passing through the dead-ball spot, or the spot where the ball is left in a side zone by a penalty.

Spot Where Run Ends
ARTICLE 8. The spot where the run ends is where the ball is declared dead or where player possession is lost during a running play. The spot where the run ends is at that point:

a.   Where the ball is declared dead by rule.
b.   Where player possession is lost on a fumble.
c.   Where a legal (or illegal) handing of the ball occurs.
d.   From where an illegal forward pass is thrown.
e.   From where a backward pass is thrown.

Spot Where Kick Ends
ARTICLE 9. A scrimmage kick that crosses the neutral zone ends at the spot where possession is gained or regained or the ball is declared dead by rule.
   Exceptions:
   1. Touchback — Basic enforcement spot: Team B's 20-yard line.
   2. When the kick ends in Team B's end zone and is not a touchback — Basic enforcement spot: Team B's one-yard line.
   3. Unsuccessful field goal attempt untouched by Team B beyond the neutral zone — Basic enforcement spot: previous spot. If the previous spot is between Team B's 20-yard line and the goal line, and the unsuccessful field goal attempt is untouched by Team B beyond the neutral zone, the spot where the kick ends is the 20-yard line.

Basic Spot
ARTICLE 10. The basic spot is the application of the "3 and 1" principle with enforcement of the penalty either from the spot where the run ends, the spot where the kick ends or the previous spot. Fouls by the team "in possession" behind the basic spot are spot fouls.
   The following are the basic spots for enforcement on running plays, forward pass plays and legal kick plays utilizing the "3 and 1" principle:
a.   The basic spot on running plays when the run ends beyond the neutral zone is **the spot where the related run ends,** and fouls by the team "in possession" behind the basic spot are **spot fouls** (10-2-2-c-1) (*Exception* 9-3-3-a & b).
b.   The basic spot on running plays when the run ends behind the neutral zone is the previous spot and fouls by the team "in possession" behind the basic spot are spot fouls (10-2-2-c-2) (*Exception* 9-3-3-a & b).
c.   The basic spot on running plays that occur when there is no neutral zone (interception runbacks, kick runbacks, fumble advances, etc.) is **the spot where the related run ends** and fouls by the team "in possession" behind the basic spot are **spot fouls** (10-2-2-c-3).
d.   The basic spot on legal forward pass plays is the previous spot, and fouls by the team "in possession" behind the basic spot are spot fouls (10-2-2-d).
   Exceptions:
   1. Defensive pass interference may be a spot foul.
   2. Illegal use of hands or holding by the offense behind the neutral zone during a legal forward pass play is not a spot foul and is penalized from the previous spot (9-3-3-a & b).
e.   The basic spot on legal kick plays before a change of possession is the previous spot, and fouls by the team in possession behind the basic spot are spot fouls (10-2-2-e *Exceptions*).

Postscrimmage Kick Spot
ARTICLE 11. The postscrimmage kick spot is the spot where the kick ends. Team B retains the ball after penalty enforcement from the postscrimmage kick spot. Fouls behind the basic spot are spot fouls (10-2-2-e-5).

SECTION 26. Tackling

ARTICLE 1. Tackling is grasping or encircling an opponent with a hand(s) or arm(s).

SECTION 27. Team and Player Designations

Teams A and B
ARTICLE 1. Team A is the team that is designated to put the ball in play and it retains that designation until the ball is next declared ready for play; Team B designates the opponents.

Offensive Team
ARTICLE 2. The offensive team is the team in possession, or the team to which the ball belongs; the defensive team is the opposing team.

Kicker
ARTICLE 3. The kicker is any player who punts, drop kicks or place kicks according to rule. He remains the kicker until he has had a reasonable time to regain his balance.

Lineman and Back
ARTICLE 4. A lineman is any player legally on his scrimmage line when the ball is snapped; a back is any player whose head does not break the plane of the line drawn through the rear-most part, other than the legs or feet, of the nearest Team A player (except the snapper) on the line of scrimmage (*Exception* 7-1-3-b-1).

Passer
ARTICLE 5. The passer is the player who throws a legal forward pass. He is a passer from the time he releases the ball until it is complete, incomplete or intercepted.

Player
ARTICLE 6. A player is any one of the partipants in the game and is subject to the rules when in bounds or out of bounds.

Runner
ARTICLE 7. The runner is a player in possession of a live ball or simulating possession of a live ball.

Snapper
ARTICLE 8. The snapper is the player who snaps the ball.

Substitute
ARTICLE 9. a. A legal substitute is a replacement for a player or a player vacancy during the interval between downs.
b. A legal incoming substitute becomes a player when he enters the field and communicates with a teammate or an official, enters the huddle, or participates in a play.
c. The player he replaces becomes a replaced player when he leaves the field.

Replaced Player
ARTICLE 10. A replaced player is one who participated during the previous down and has been replaced by a substitute.

Player Vacancy
ARTICLE 11. A player vacancy occurs when a team has fewer than 11 players in the game.

Disqualified Player
ARTICLE 12. A disqualified player is one who is declared ineligible for further participation in the game.

SECTION 28. Tripping

ARTICLE 1. Tripping is using the lower leg or foot to obstruct an opponent (except the runner) below the knees.

SECTION 29. Timing Devices

Game Clock
ARTICLE 1. Any device under the direction of the appropriate judge used to time the 60 minutes of the game.

25-Second Clock
ARTICLE 2. Any device under the direction of the appropriate official to time the 25 seconds between the ready for play and the ball being put in play. The type of device is determined by the game management.

SECTION 30. Play Classification

Forward Pass Play
ARTICLE 1. A legal forward pass play is the interval between the snap and when a legal forward pass is complete, incomplete or intercepted.

Free Kick Play
ARTICLE 2. A free kick play is the interval from the time the ball is legally kicked until it comes into player possession or the ball is declared dead by rule.

Scrimmage Kick Play and Field Goal Play
ARTICLE 3. A scrimmage kick play or field goal play is the interval between the snap and when a scrimmage kick comes into player possession or the ball is declared dead by rule.

Running Play
ARTICLE 4. A running play is any live-ball action other than that which occurs before player possession is reestablished during a free kick play, a scrimmage kick play, or a legal forward pass play.
a. A running play includes the spot where the run ends and the interval of any subsequent fumble or backward or illegal pass from the time the run ends until possession is gained, regained or the ball is declared dead by rule.
    1. There may be more than one running play during a down if player possession is gained or regained beyond the neutral zone.

2. There may not be more than one running play behind the neutral zone if no change of team possession occurs, and the basic spot is the previous spot (see Rule 10-2-2-c-2).
b. A run is that segment of a running play before player possession is lost.

SECTION 31. Field Areas

The Field
ARTICLE 1. The field is the area within the limit lines and includes the limit lines and team areas and the space above it (*Exception:* Enclosures over the field).

Field of Play
ARTICLE 2. The field of play is the area within the boundary lines other than the end zones.

End Zones
ARTICLE 3. The end zones are the 10-yard areas at both ends of the field between the end lines and the goal lines. The goal lines and goal line pylons are in the end zone and a team's end zone is the one they are defending.

Playing Surface
ARTICLE 4. The playing surface is the material or substance within the field.

Playing Enclosure
ARTICLE 5. The playing enclosure is that area bounded by the stadium, dome, stands, fences or other structures. (*Exception:* Scoreboards are not considered within the playing enclosure.)

RULE 3

Periods, Time Factors and Substitutions

SECTION 1. Start of Each Period

First and Third Periods
ARTICLE 1. Each half shall start with a kickoff. Three minutes before the scheduled starting time the referee shall toss a coin at midfield in the presence of the field captains of the opposing teams, first designating which field captain shall call the fall of the coin.

During the coin toss, each team shall remain in the area between the sideline and in-bounds line nearest its team area or in the team area.
a.   The winner of the toss shall choose one of the following options for the first or second half at the beginning of the half selected.
   1. To designate which team shall kick off.
   2. To designate which goal line his team shall defend.
b.   The loser shall choose one of the above options for the half the winner of the toss did not select.
c.   The team not having the choice of options for a half shall exercise the option not chosen by the opponent.
d.   If the winner of the toss selects the second half option, the referee shall use [S10].

Second and Fourth Periods
ARTICLE 2. Between the first and second periods and also between the third and fourth periods, the teams shall defend opposite goal lines.
a.   The ball shall be relocated at a spot corresponding exactly, in relation to goal lines and sidelines, to its location at the end of the preceding period.
b.   Possession of the ball, the number of the down and the distance to be gained shall remain unchanged.

Extra Periods
ARTICLE 3. a. When it is necessary to determine a champion, or a team's progress in post-season, extra periods of 15 minutes each shall be played to decide a tied game.
b.   The Referee shall toss a coin in the presence of field captains of both teams. The winner of the toss shall elect to:
   i. designate which team shall kick-off, OR
   ii. designate which goal-line his team will defend.

The loser of the toss shall elect one of the options the winner does not select.

c.   The game shall end when one team scores. That team shall be declared the winner.

d.   If the first score is a touchdown, no extra point attempt will be permitted.

SECTION 2. Playing Time and Intermissions

Length of Periods and Intermissions
ARTICLE 1. The total playing time in a collegiate game shall be 60 minutes divided into four periods of 15 minutes each, with one-minute intermissions between the first and second periods (first half) and between the third and fourth periods (second half).

a.   No period shall end until the ball is dead.

b.   The intermission between halves shall be 20 minutes.

Timing Adjustments
ARTICLE 2. Before the game starts, playing time may be shortened by mutual agreement of the opposing field captains or may be arbitrarily shortened by the referee if he is of the opinion that darkness may interfere with the game. In either of such cases, the four periods must be of equal length.

a.   Anytime during the game, the playing time of any remaining period or periods may be shortened by mutual agreement of the opposing field captains and the referee.

b.   Timing errors on the game clock, or by an official, may be corrected by the referee.

Extension of Periods
ARTICLE 3. A period shall be extended until a down free from live-ball fouls not penalized as dead-ball fouls has been played when:

a.   A penalty is accepted for a live-ball foul(s) not penalized as a dead-ball foul that occurs during a down in which time expires.

b.   An inadvertent whistle is sounded during a down in which time expires.

c.   A touchdown is scored during a down in which time expires. (*Exception:* If the winner of the game has been decided and both field captains agree to forego the try, the period is not extended.)

d.   Offsetting fouls occur during a down in which time expires.

Game Clock
ARTICLE 4. a. Playing time shall be kept with a game clock that may be either a stop watch operated by the field judge, line judge or back judge, or a game clock operated by an assistant under the direction of the appropriate judge.

b.   The 25 seconds between the ready for play and the ball being put in play shall be timed with a watch operated by the appropriate official or 25-second clocks at each end of the playing enclosure operated by an assistant under the direction of the appropriate official. The use of a 25-second clock shall be determined by the game management.

When Clock Starts
ARTICLE 5. Following a free kick the game clock shall be started when the ball is legally touched in the field of play or crosses the goal line after being legally touched by Team B in its end zone. On a scrimmage down, the game clock shall be started when the ball is snapped or on prior signal by the referee. The clock shall not run during a try or during an extension of a period.

a. The referee signals, sounds his whistle and the game clock starts when the ball is ready for play, if it was stopped:
    1. When Team A is awarded a first down (*Exception:* 3-2-5-b-2).
    2. For a referee's timeout for an injured player or official.
    3. At the referee's discretion (see Rule 3-4-3).
    4. To complete a penalty (see Rule 3-2-5-e).
    5. For an inadvertent whistle (except on a free kick).
    6. For a head coach's conference.
b. The referee does NOT signal and the game clock starts when the ball is put in play, if it was stopped:
    1. By a charged team timeout, a score, a touchback, an incompleted forward pass, or a live ball going out of bounds.
    2. To award a first down to Team B, or when after a kick Team A is awarded a first down. The referee shall not declare the ball ready for play until both teams have had reasonable opportunity to complete their substitutions.
    3. To complete a penalty for an infraction by the defensive team with less than 25 seconds remaining in the second and fourth periods (*Exception:* Rule 3-4-3).
    4. When a 7-1-3-a-4 false start *Exception* occurs.
    5. For a 3-4-2-a *Exception.*
c. If incidents in (a), above, occur in conjunction with a charged team timeout or any other incident following which the clock would not start until the ball is put in play, it shall be started when the ball is put in play.
d. If the clock has been stopped for incidents in (a), above, and then subsequently is stopped for a radio or TV timeout, the game clock shall start when the ball is ready for play.
e. If the clock was stopped to complete a penalty, it shall be started when the ball is declared ready for play unless 3-4-3 or A.R. 4 is invoked. If the clock had been stopped otherwise by rule, it shall be started on the snap.

When Clock Stops
ARTICLE 6. The game clock shall be stopped when each period ends. Any official may signal timeout when the rules provide for stopping the clock or when a timeout is charged to a team or to the referee. (*Exception:* 3-3-4-e). Other officials should repeat timeout signals.

SECTION 3. Timeouts

How Charged
ARTICLE 1. a. The referee shall declare a timeout when he suspends play for any reason. Each timeout shall be charged to one of the teams or designated as referee's timeout.
b. When a team's timeouts are exhausted and it requests a timeout with the 25-second clock running, the official should not acknowledge the request, interrupt the 25-second count or stop the game clock.
c. During a timeout, players shall not practice with a ball on the field of play. (*Exception:* During the halftime intermission.)

Timeout
ARTICLE 2. The referee shall declare a timeout:
a. When a touchdown, field goal, touchback or safety is scored.
b. When an injury timeout is allowed.
c. When the clock is stopped to complete a penalty.
d. When a live ball goes out of bounds or is declared out of bounds.
e. When a forward pass becomes incomplete.
f. When Team A or B is awarded a first down.
g. When an inadvertent whistle is sounded.
h. When a head coach's conference is requested.
i. When a radio or TV timeout is allowed.
j. When an unfair noise timeout is required.
k. When there is a first-down measurement.
l. When a delay is caused by both teams.
m. When a charged timeout is requested.

Referee's Discretionary Timeout
ARTICLE 3. a. The referee may temporarily suspend the game when conditions warrant such action. The referee may declare and charge himself with a timeout for any contingency not elsewhere covered by the rules.
b. When the game is stopped by actions of a person(s) not subject to the rules or for any other reasons not in the rules and cannot continue, the referee shall:
   1. Suspend play and direct the players to their team areas.
   2. Refer the problem to those responsible for the game's management.
   3. Resume the game when he determines conditions are satisfactory.
c. If a game may not be resumed immediately after Rule 3-3-3-a & b suspensions, it shall be terminated or resumed at a later time only by mutual consent of both teams.
d. A suspended game, if resumed, will begin with the same time remaining and under the identical conditions of down, distance and field position.
e. The game is a no-contest if there is not mutual consent of both teams to resume or terminate the game. (*Exception:* Conference or league regulations.)
f. The referee's discretionary timeout also applies to the following play situations:
   1. When there is undue delay by officials in placing the ball for the next snap.
   2. When there is a consultation with team captains.
   3. When conditions warrant temporary suspension.
   4. When the offensive team cannot hear its signals because of crowd noise or noise created by persons subject to the rules.

      Administrative procedures for unfair noise:
      a. When unable to communicate signals to teammates because of unfair noise, a quarterback may raise his hands and look to the referee to request a legal delay.
      b. The referee may charge himself with a timeout and the offensive team may huddle. The referee may deny the request by pointing toward the defensive team's goal line.
      c. When the offensive team returns to the line of scrimmage, the game clock will start on the snap. The referee shall declare the ball ready for play by sounding his whistle. The 25-second clock is not in operation.
      d. Should the quarterback, during the game, subsequently request a second legal delay by raising his hands and looking to the referee, the referee will again charge himself with a timeout if, in his opinion, the unfair noise makes it impossible to hear offensive signals.

    e. The referee will then request the defensive captain to ask the crowd/persons subject to the rules for quiet. This signals the public address announcer to request cooperation and courtesy to the offensive team. The announcer will state that the defensive team will be charged a timeout for the next noise infraction.

    f. When the offensive team returns to the line of scrimmage, the game clock will start on the snap. The referee shall declare the ball ready for play by sounding his whistle. The 25-second clock is not in operation.

    g. If the quarterback again, during the game, indicates by raising his hands and looking to the referee to request a legal delay because his signals are not audible and the referee agrees, a team timeout will be charged to the defensive team.

    h. Following this timeout, the defensive team will be charged an additional team timeout for each subsequent unsuccessful attempt to start play. Only one timeout may be charged during the interval between downs.

    i. If the 25-second clock has been stopped twice for unfair noise violations against the same team, any subsequent stopping of the 25-second clock because of unfair noise against the same team will result in a charged timeout, or a delay penalty, if all the offending team's timeouts have been used.

Charged Team Timeouts

ARTICLE 4. The referee shall allow a charged team timeout when requested by any player or when an obviously injured player is not replaced.

a. Each team is entitled to three charged team timeouts during each half without penalty.

b. Consecutive charged team timeouts during an interval between downs shall not be allowed the same team (*Exceptions:* 1-4-4, 1-4-5, 3-3-4-e, 3-3-5 and 9-1-5-a).

c. After the ball is declared dead and before the snap, a legal substitue may request a timeout if he is within 15 yards of the ball.

d. A player who participated during the previous down may request a timeout between the time of the ready for play and the snap without being within 15 yards of the ball.

e. A player or incoming substitute may request a conference with the referee if the coach believes a rule has been improperly enforced. If the rule enforcement is not changed, the coach's team will be charged a timeout, or a delay penalty if all timeouts have been used.

    1. Only the referee may stop the clock for a coach's conference.

    2. A request for a conference must be requested before the ball is snapped or free-kicked for the next play and before the end of the second and fourth period.

Injury Timeout

ARTICLE 5. a. In the event of an obviously injured player, the referee may charge himself with a timeout, provided the player for whom the timeout is taken is removed from the game for at least one down. Otherwise his team will be charged with a team timeout. After a team's charged timeouts have been exhausted, the injured player must leave for one down. The referee may charge himself with a timeout for an injured official.

b. Any official may stop the clock for an injured player.

c. To curtail a possible time-gaining advantage by feigning injuries, attention is directed to the strongly worded statement in "The Football Code" concerning the feigning of any injury.

d.   An injury timeout may follow a charged team timeout (3-3-5).

Violation Timeouts
ARTICLE 6. For noncompliance with 1-4-4, 1-4-5, 3-3-4-e or 9-1-5-a during a down, a timeout shall be charged to a team at the succeeding spot (see Rule 3-4-2-b).

Length of Timeouts
ARTICLE 7. a. A charged team timeout requested by any player shall not exceed one minute and 30 seconds. Other timeouts shall be no longer than the referee deems necessary to fulfill the purpose for which they are declared including a radio or TV timeout, but any timeout may be extended by the referee for the benefit of a seriously injured player.
b.   If the team charged with a one-minute 30-second team timeout wishes to resume play before the expiration of one minute and its opponent indicates readiness, the referee will declare the ball ready for play.
c.   The length of a referee's timeouts depend on the circumstances of each timeout.
d.   The field captain must exercise his penalty option before he or a teammate consults with his coach on a sideline during a timeout.

Referee's Notification
ARTICLE 8. The referee shall notify both teams 30 seconds before a charged team timeout expires and five seconds later shall declare the ball ready for play.
a.   When a third timeout is charged to a team in either half, the referee shall notify the field captain and head coach of that team.
b.   Unless a game clock is the official timepiece, the referee also shall inform each field captain and head coach when approximately two minutes of playing time remain in each half. He may order the clock stopped for that purpose.
c.   If a visible game clock is not the official timing device during the last two minutes of each half, the referee or his representative shall notify each captain and head coach of the time remaining each time the clock is stopped by rule. Also, a representative may leave the team area along the limit line to relay timing information under these conditions.

SECTION 4. Delays

Delaying the Start of a Half
ARTICLE 1. a. Each team shall have its players on the field for the opening play at the scheduled time for the beginning of each half.

PENALTY—15 yards [S7 and S21].

b.   The home management is responsible for clearing the field of play and end zones at the beginning of each half so the periods may start at the scheduled time. Bands, speeches, presentations, homecoming and similar activities are under the jurisdiction of home management and a prompt start of each half is mandatory.

PENALTY—10 yards [S7 and S21].

Exception: The referee may waive the penalty for circumstances beyond the control of the home management.

Illegal Delay of the Game
ARTICLE 2. a. The ball shall be declared ready for play consistently throughout the game by the referee when the officials are in position. Consuming more than 25 seconds to put the ball in play after it is declared ready for play is an illegal delay. (*Exceptions:* When the 25-second count is interrupted by circumstances beyond the control of either team, or unfair noise situations occur, a new 25-second count shall be started and the game clock shall start on the snap.)
b.   Illegal delay also includes:
1.   Crawling or deliberately advancing the ball after it is dead.
2.   When a team has expended its three timeouts and commits a 1-4-4, 1-4-5, 3-3-4-e or 9-1-5-a infraction.

PENALTY—5 yards [S7 and S21].

Unfair Game Clock Tactics
ARTICLE 3. The referee shall order the game clock started or stopped whenever, in his opinion, either team is trying to conserve or consume playing time by tactics obviously unfair. This includes starting the clock on the snap if the foul is by the team ahead in the score and any illegal forward pass or illegal touching that conserves time for Team A.

PENALTY—5 yards [S7 and S21].

SECTION 5. Substitutions

Substitution Procedures
ARTICLE 1. Any number of legal substitutes for either team may enter the game between periods, after a score or try, or during the interval between downs only for the purpose of replacing a player(s).

PENALTY—5 yards [S22].

Legal Substitutions
ARTICLE 2. A legal substitute may replace a player or fill a player vacancy provided none of the following restrictions is violated:
a.   No incoming substitute or replaced player shall be on the field while the ball is in play.
b.   An incoming legal substitute must enter the field directly from his team area and a substitute or player leaving must depart at the sideline nearest his team area. A replaced player must also leave at the sideline nearest his team area.
c.   Substitutes who become players must remain in the game for one play and replaced players must remain out of the game for one play except during the interval between periods, after a score, or when a timeout has been charged to a team, or to the referee.
d.   Teams shall have no more than 3 American or Canadian players on the field at any one time. These are defined as players who still hold American or Canadian nationality and/or passport. A team is allowed to suit-up 5 such players on the day of the game, but only three shall be part of any one play on the field at any one time.

PENALTY—15 yards from previous spot plus loss of down [22]

Regulations for Youth and Junior Teams
ARTICLE 3. Youth and Junior Teams may adopt more liberal substitution regulations when mutually agreed or when authorized by their association, league of federation.

RULE 4

Ball in Play,
Dead Ball,
Out of Bounds

SECTION 1. Ball in Play—Dead Ball

Dead Ball Becomes Alive
ARTICLE 1. After a dead ball has been declared ready for play, it becomes a live ball when it is legally snapped, or free kicked legally. A ball snapped or free kicked before the ready for play shall be whistled by the official.

Live Ball Becomes Dead
ARTICLE 2. a. A live ball becomes a dead ball as provided in the rules or when an official sounds his whistle (even though inadvertently), or otherwise declares the ball dead.
b. An official sounds his whistle inadvertently during a down when:
   1. A live ball in player possession or loose is in or behind the neutral zone and there has been no change of team possession — replay the down, if not in conflict with other rules.
   2. A live ball is beyond the neutral zone and there has been no change of team possession:
      (a) Ball in player possession — Option: Team A may elect to put the ball in play where declared dead or replay the down, if not in conflict with other rules.
      (b) Loose following a fumble, backward pass or illegal forward pass — return to the spot where last possessed, if not in conflict with other rules.
   3. Following a change of team possession, a live ball is:
      (a) In player possession — ball shall be put in play where declared dead, if not in conflict with other rules.
      (b) Loose following a fumble, backward pass or illegal forward pass — return to the spot where last possessed, if not in conflict with other rules.
   4. During a legal forward pass or a free or scrimmage kick, the ball is returned to the previous spot and the down replayed, if not in conflict with other rules.
   5. A live ball not in player possession touches anything in bounds other than the ground, a player or an official, the inadvertent whistle rule applies.
   6. Anyone other than a player or an official interferes in any way other than with a live ball not in player possession, the inadvertent whistle rule applies.

NOTE: If a foul occurs during any of the above downs, the penalty shall be administered as in any other play situation. Enforce postscrimmage kick fouls from the previous spot.

Ball Declared Dead
ARTICLE 3. A live ball becomes dead and an official shall sound his whistle or declare it dead:

a. When it goes out of bounds, when a runner is out of bounds or when a runner is so held that his forward progress is stopped.
b. When any part of the runner's body, except his hand or foot, touches the ground or when the runner is tackled or otherwise falls and loses possession of the ball as he contacts the ground with any part of his body, except his hand or foot. (*Exception:* The ball remains alive when an offensive player has simulated a kick or is in position to kick the ball held for a place kick by a teammate. The ball may be kicked, passed or advanced.)
c. When a touchdown, touchback, safety, field goal, or successful try occurs, or when Team A completes an illegal forward pass in Team B's end zone, or Team A completes a forward pass to an ineligible player in Team B's end zone.
d. When during a try, Team B obtains possession of the ball or when it becomes certain that a scrimmage kick on a try will not score the point.
e. When a player of the kicking team catches or recovers any free kick or a scrimmage kick that is beyond the neutral zone; when a free kick or scrimmage kick comes to rest and no player attempts to secure it; when a free kick or scrimmage kick is caught or recovered by any player following a valid, invalid or illegal signal (any waving signal) for a fair catch beyond the neutral zone, or when a return kick is made.
f. When a forward pass strikes the ground.
g. When a live ball not in player possession touches anything in bounds other than a player, official or the ground.
h. When a simultaneous catch or recovery of a live ball is made in bounds by opposing players.
i. When the ball becomes illegal while in play, inadvertent whistle provisions apply.

Ball Ready For Play
ARTICLE 4. No player shall put the ball in play until it is declared ready for play.

PENALTY — 5 yards from the spot where the ball should have been put in play legally [S7 and S19].

25-Second Count
ARTICLE 5. The ball shall be put in play within 25 seconds after it is declared ready for play, unless, during that interval, play is suspended. If play is suspended, the 25-second count will start again (*Exception:* Unfair crowd noise situations.)

PENALTY—5 yards [S7 and S21].

SECTION 2. Out of Bounds

Player Out of Bounds
ARTICLE 1. A player is out of bounds when any part of his person touches anything, other than another player or game official, on or outside a boundary line. A player who touches a pylon is out of bounds behind the goal line.

Held Ball Out of Bounds
ARTICLE 2. A ball in player possession is out of bounds when either the ball or any part of the runner touches the ground or anything else that is on or outside a boundary line except another player or game official.

Ball Out of Bounds
ARTICLE 3. A ball not in player possession, other than a kick that scores a goal, is out of bounds when it touches the ground, a player or anything else that is on or outside a boundary line. A ball that touches a pylon is out of bounds behind the goal line.

Out of Bounds at Crossing Point
ARTICLE 4. a. If a live ball not in player possession crosses a boundary line and is then declared out of bounds, it is out of bounds at the crossing point.
b. If the ball is in bounds when the runner is ruled out of bounds, the dead-ball spot is directly under the foremost part of the ball.
c. If the ball is on or above the out-of-bounds territory when the runner is ruled out of bounds, the dead-ball spot is directly under the foremost part of the ball.
d. A touchdown may be scored if the ball is in bounds and has broken the plane of the goal line before or simultaneously with the runner's going out of bounds.
e. An eligible receiver who is in the opponent's end zone and contacting the ground is credited with a completion if he reaches over the sideline or end line and catches a legal pass.

Out of Bounds at Forward Point
ARTICLE 5. If a live ball is declared out of bounds and the ball does not cross a boundary line, it is out of bounds at the ball's most forward point when it was declared dead.

RULE 5

Series of Downs, Line to Gain

SECTION 1. A Series: Started, Broken, Renewed

When to Award Series

ARTICLE 1. a. A series of four consecutive scrimmage downs shall be awarded to the team that is next to put the ball in play by a snap following a free kick, touchback, fair catch or change in team possession.

b. A new series shall be awarded to Team A if it is in legal possession of the ball on or beyond its line to gain.

c. A new series shall be awarded to Team B if, after fourth down, Team A has failed to earn a first down.

d. A new series shall be awarded to Team B if A's scrimmage kick goes out of bounds or comes to rest and no player attempts to secure it.

e. A new series shall be awarded to the team in legal possession:
  1. If a change of team possession occurs during the down.
  2. If a player of Team B first touches a scrimmage kick that has crossed the neutral zone. (*Exception:* When a penalty for a foul by either team is accepted and the down is replayed.)
  3. If an accepted penalty awards the ball to the offended team.
  4. If an accepted penalty mandates a first down.

Line to Gain

ARTICLE 2. The line to gain for a series shall be established 10 yards in advance of the most forward point of the ball; but if this line is in the opponents' end zone, the goal line becomes the line to gain.

Measurement of Distance

ARTICLE 3. a. The most forward point of the ball when declared dead between the goal lines shall be the determining point in measuring distance gained or lost by either team during any down. The ball shall always be placed with its length axis parallel to the sideline before measuring.

b. Unnecessary measurements to determine first downs shall not be requested, but any doubtful distance should be measured without request.

Continuity of Downs Broken
ARTICLE 4. The continuity of a series of downs is broken when:
a. Team possession of the ball changes during a down.
b. A player of Team B touches a scrimmage kick that has crossed the neutral zone.
c. A kick goes out of bounds.
d. A kick comes to rest and no player attempts to secure it.
e. At the end of a down, Team A has earned a first down. Any down may be repeated if so provided by the rules.
f. After fourth down, Team A has failed to earn a first down.

SECTION 2. Down and Possession After a Penalty

Foul During Free Kick
ARTICLE 1. When a scrimmage follows the penalty for a foul committed during a free kick, the down and distance established by that penalty shall be first down with 10 yards to gain.

Penalty Resulting in First Down
ARTICLE 2. It is a first down with 10 yards to gain:
a. After a penalty that leaves the ball in possession of Team A beyond its line to gain.
b. After a pass interference penalty has awarded the ball to Team A between the goal lines.
c. When a penalty stipulates a first down.

Foul Before Change of Team Possession
ARTICLE 3. After a distance penalty between the goal lines, incurred during a scrimmage down and before any change of team possession during that down, the ball belongs to Team A and the down shall be repeated unless the penalty also involves loss of a down, stipulates a first down, or leaves the ball on or beyond the line to gain (*Exception:* 10-2-2-e-5).
   If the penalty involves loss of a down, the down shall count as one of the four in that series.

Foul After Change of Team Possession
ARTICLE 4. If a distance penalty is accepted for a foul incurred during a down after change of team possession, the ball belongs to the team in possession when the foul occurred. The down and distance established by any distance penalty incurred after change of team possession during that down shall be first down with 10 yards to gain. (*Exception:* Live-ball fouls penalized as dead-ball fouls).

Penalty Declined
ARTICLE 5. If a penalty is declined, the number of the next down shall be whatever it would have been if that foul had not occurred.

Foul Between Downs
ARTICLE 6. After a distance penalty incurred between downs, the number of the next down shall be the same as that established before the foul occurred unless enforcement for a foul by Team B leaves the ball on or beyond the line to gain or a foul requires a first down.

Foul Between Series
ARTICLE 7. A scrimmage following a penalty incurred after a series ends and before the next series begins shall be first down, but the line to gain shall be established before the penalty is enforced.

Fouls by Both Teams
ARTICLE 8. If offsetting fouls occur during a down, that down shall be repeated. (*Exception:* 10-1-4). If canceling fouls occur between successive downs, the next down shall be the same as it would have been had no fouls occurred.

Fouls During a Loose Ball
ARTICLE 9. Fouls when the ball is loose shall be penalized from the basic or previous spot (10-2-2-c, d, e & f).

   If a team had not fouled prior to gaining possession of a loose ball or forward pass, it may retain possession by refusing any penalty for a foul by an opponent.

Rule Decisions Final
ARTICLE 10. No rule decision may be changed after the ball is next legally snapped or legally free kicked.

RULE 6

Kicks

SECTION 1. Free Kicks

Restraining Lines
ARTICLE 1. For any free kick formation, the kicking team's restraining line shall be the yard line through the most forward point from which the ball shall be kicked, and the receiving team's restraining line shall be the yard line 10 yards beyond that point. Unless relocated by a penalty, the kicking team's restraining line on a kickoff shall be its 40-yard line and for a free kick after a safety, its 20-yard line.

Free Kick Formation
ARTICLE 2. A ball from a free kick formation must be kicked legally and from some point on Team A's restraining line and on or between the in-bounds lines. After the ball is ready for play and for any reason it falls from the tee, Team A shall not kick the ball and the official shall sound his whistle immediately. When the ball is kicked:
a. All players of each team must be in bounds.
b. Each Team A player except the holder and kicker of a place kick must be behind the ball. After a safety, when a punt or drop kick is used, the ball shall be kicked within one yard behind the kicking team's restraining line.
c. All Team B players must be behind their restraining line.
d. At least five Team B players must be within five yards of their restraining line.
e. Team A substitutes may not touch a kick if they enter the field after the ball is declared ready for play.
f. A Team A player who voluntarily goes out of bounds during the kick may not return in bounds during the down.
PENALTY—5 yards from previous spot [S18 or S19].

Free Kick Recovery
ARTICLE 3. A Team A player may touch a free kicked ball:
a. After it touches a Team B player.
b. After it breaks the plane of and remains beyond Team B's restraining line.

c. After it touches any player, the ground or an official beyond Team B's restraining line.

Thereafter, all players of Team A become eligible to touch, recover or catch the kick (*Exception:* 6-1-2-e & f). Illegal touching of a free kick is a violation that, when the ball becomes dead, gives the receiving team the privilege of taking the ball at the spot of the violation. However, if a penalty incurred by either team before the ball becomes dead is accepted, this privilege is canceled.

Forced Touching Disregarded
ARTICLE 4. a. An in-bounds player pushed or blocked by an opponent into a free kick is not, while in bounds, deemed to have touched the kick.
b. An in-bounds player touched by a ball batted by an opponent is not deemed to have touched the ball.

Free Kick at Rest
ARTICLE 5. If a free kick comes to rest in bounds and no player attempts to secure it, the ball becomes dead and belongs to the receiving team at the dead-ball spot.

Free Kick Caught or Recovered
ARTICLE 6. If a free kick is caught or recovered by a player of the receiving team, the ball continues in play (*Exceptions:* 6-1-7, 6-5-1 and 2, and 4-1-3-e). If caught or recovered by a player of the kicking team, the ball becomes dead.

Touching Ground On or Beyond Goal Lines
ARTICLE 7. The ball becomes dead and belongs to the team defending its goal line when a free kick is untouched by Team B prior to touching the ground on or behind Team B's goal line.

SECTION 2. Free Kick Out of Bounds

Kicking Team
ARTICLE 1. A free kick out of bounds between the goal lines untouched in bounds by a player of Team B is a foul.

PENALTY—Repeat kick 5 yards behind previous spot [S19] .

Receiving Team
ARTICLE 2. When a free kick goes out of bounds between the goal lines, the ball belongs to the receiving team at the in-bounds spot. When a free kick goes out of bounds behind the goal line, the ball belongs to the team defending that goal line.

SECTION 3. Scrimmage Kicks

Fails to Cross Neutral Zone
ARTICLE 1. Except during a try, a scrimmage kick behind the neutral zone continues in play. All players may catch or recover the ball behind the neutral zone and advance it.

Crosses the Neutral Zone

ARTICLE 2. a. No in-bounds player of the kicking team shall touch a scrimmage kick beyond the neutral zone before it touches an opponent. Such illegal touching is a violation that, when the ball becomes dead, gives the receiving team the privilege of taking the ball at the spot of the violation. However, if a penalty incurred by either team before the ball becomes dead is accepted, this privilege is canceled. (*Exceptions:* 2-25-11, 8-4-2-b and 10-2-2-e-5).

b. Blocking of a kick that occurs in the vicinity of the neutral zone is ruled as having occurred within or behind that zone.

All Become Eligible

ARTICLE 3. When a scrimmage kick that has crossed the neutral zone touches a player of the receiving team who is in bounds, any player may catch or recover the ball.

Forced Touching Disregarded

ARTICLE 4. a. A player pushed or blocked by an opponent into a scrimmage kick that has crossed the neutral zone, shall not, while in bounds, be deemed to have touched the kick.

b. An in-bounds player touched by a ball batted by an opponent is not deemed to have touched the ball.

Catch or Recovery by Receiving Team

ARTICLE 5. If a scrimmage kick is caught or recovered by a player of the receiving team, the ball continues in play. (*Exception:* 6-3-9, 6-5-1 and 2, and 4-1-3-e).

Catch or Recovery by Kicking Team

ARTICLE 6. a. If a player of the kicking team catches or recovers a scrimmage kick beyond the neutral zone, the ball becomes dead.

b. When opposing players, each eligible to touch the ball, simultaneously recover a rolling kick or catch a scrimmage kick, this simultaneous possession makes the ball dead. A kick declared dead in joint possession of opposing players is awarded to the receiving team (2-2-8) (4-1-3-i).

Out of Bounds Between Goal Lines or at Rest

ARTICLE 7. If a scrimmage kick goes out of bounds between the goal lines, or comes to rest in bounds and no player attempts to secure it, the ball becomes dead and belongs to the receiving team at the dead-ball spot (*Exception:* 8-4-2-b).

Out of Bounds Behind Goal Line

ARTICLE 8. If a scrimmage kick (other than one that scores a field goal) goes out of bounds behind a goal line, the ball becomes dead and belongs to the team defending that goal line (*Exception:* 8-4-2-b).

Touching Ground On or Behind Goal

ARTICLE 9. The ball becomes dead and belongs to the team defending its goal line when a scrimmage kick is untouched by Team B beyond the neutral zone prior to touching the ground on or behind Team B's goal line (*Exception:* 8-4-2-b).

Legal Kick

ARTICLE 10. A legal scrimmage kick is a punt, drop kick or place kick made according to the rules. A return kick is an illegal kick and a live ball foul that causes the ball to become dead.

PENALTY—For an illegal kick 5 yards [S31].

Loose Behind the Goal Line
ARTICLE 11. If a Team A player bats a loose ball behind Team B's goal line during a scrimmage kick, it is a live-ball foul (*Exception:* 8-4-2-b).

PENALTY—Touchback [S7 and S31].

SECTION 4. Opportunity to Catch a Kick

Interference with Opportunity
ARTICLE 1. A player of the receiving team who is within the boundary lines and is so located that he could have caught a free kick or a scrimmage kick that is beyond the neutral zone while such kick is in flight must be given an unmolested opportunity to catch the kick.
a. No player of the kicking team may be within two yards of a player positioned to catch a free or scrimmage kick while the ball is in a downward flight.
b. This protection terminates when the kick is touched by any player of Team B or the ground.
c. If contact with a potential receiver is the result of a player being blocked or pushed by an opponent, it is not a foul.
d. It is not a foul if a member of the kicking team is blocked to within two yards of the receiver when the ball is on its downward flight.
e. It is a contact foul if the kicking team contacts the potential receiver prior to, or simultaneous with, his first touching of the ball.

PENALTY— For foul between goal lines: receiving team's ball, first down, 15 yards beyond spot of foul for contact foul and 5 yards for noncontact foul. For foul behind goal line: award touchback and penalize from succeeding spot [S33]. Flagrant offenders shall be disqualified.

SECTION 5. Fair Catch

Dead Where Caught
ARTICLE 1. a. When a Team B player makes a fair catch, the ball becomes dead where caught and belongs to Team B at that spot.
b. Rules pertaining to a fair catch apply only when a scrimmage kick crosses the neutral zone or during free kicks.
c. The purpose of the fair catch provision is to protect the receiver who, by his fair catch signal, agrees he or a teammate will not advance after the catch.
d. The ball shall be put in play by a snap by the receiving team at the spot of the catch, if the ball is caught.

No Advance
ARTICLE 2. No Team B player shall carry a caught or recovered ball more than two steps in any direction following a valid, invalid or illegal fair catch signal by any Team B player.

PENALTY—5 yards from basic spot. Penalize as dead ball foul [S7 and S21].

Illegal Signals
ARTICLE 3. a. During a down in which a kick is made, no player of Team B shall make any illegal fair catch signal during a free kick or beyond the neutral zone during a scrimmage kick.

b. A catch following a valid illegal signal is a fair catch. The ball is dead where caught unless the signal follows the catch.
c. Fouls for illegal signals beyond the neutral zone apply only to Team B.
d. An illegal signal beyond the neutral zone is possible only when the ball has crossed the neutral zone (2-15-7).

> **PENALTY—Free kick: receiving team's ball 15 yards from spot of foul (10-2-2-e) [S32].**
> **Scrimmage kick: receiving team's ball 15 yards from basic spot (10-2-2-e-5) [S32].**

Illegal Block
ARTICLE 4. A player of Team B who has made a valid, invalid or illegal signal for a fair catch and does not touch the ball shall not block or foul an opponent during that down.

PENALTY— Free kick: receiving team's ball 15 yards from spot of foul (10-2-2-e) [S38, S39 or S40].
Scrimmage kick: receiving team's ball 15 yards from basic spot (10-2-2-e-5) [S38, S39 or S40].

No Tackling
ARTICLE 5. No player of the kicking team shall tackle or block an opponent who has completed a fair catch. Only the player making a fair catch signal has this protection.

PENALTY— Receiving team's ball 15 yards from succeeding spot [S7 and S38].

RULE 7

Snapping and Passing the Ball

SECTION 1. The Scrimmage

Starting with a Snap
ARTICLE 1. The ball shall be put in play by a legal snap unless the rules provide for a legal free kick.

PENALTY—5 yards from previous spot. Penalize as dead-ball foul [S7 and S19].

Not in a Side Zone
ARTICLE 2. The ball may not be snapped in a side zone. If the starting point for any scrimmage down is in a side zone, it shall be transferred to the in-bounds spot.

Offensive Team Requirements
ARTICLE 3. The offensive requirements for a scrimmage are as follows:

a. **Before the ball is snapped:**
   1. The snapper, after assuming his position for the succeeding snap and adjusting the ball, may neither move nor change the position of the ball in a manner simulating the beginning of a play. An infraction of this provision may be penalized whether or not the ball is snapped and the penalty for any resultant offsides or contact foul by an opponent shall be canceled. Excessive tilting is not a foul until the snap and is a live-ball foul [S7 and S19].
   2. After the ball is ready for play and before the snap, each player or entering substitute of Team A must have been within 15 yards of the ball [S19].
   3. No player of the offensive team shall make a false start including contacting an opponent after the ball is ready for play or be in or beyond the neutral zone after the snapper touches the ball and before the snap.
   (*Exceptions:* Does not apply to substitutes and replaced players or offensive players in a scrimmage kick formation who, after the snapper touches the ball, point at opponents and break the neutral zone with their hand(s).) A false start includes:
   (a) Feigning a charge.
   (b) A shift or movement that simulates the beginning of a play. This includes the snapper, who after assuming a position for the succeeding snap and touching the ball, moves to another position.

54

(c) A lineman between the snapper and the player on the end of the line or a player other than the snapper wearing a number 50-79, after having placed a hand(s) on or near the ground, moves his hand(s), or makes any quick movement.

(d) An offensive player, neither legally in the backfield nor legally on the line of scrimmage after having placed a hand(s) on or near the ground, moves his hand(s) or makes any quick movement.

4. It is not a false start if any player on the line of scrimmage moves when threatened by a Team B player in the neutral zone. The threatened Team A player may not enter the neutral zone.

5. An official shall sound his whistle when:
   (a) There is a false start.
   (b) An offensive player is in or beyond the neutral zone after the snapper touches the ball.
   (c) A Team A player moves into the neutral zone when threatened by a Team B player in the neutral zone.
   (d) A 7-1-3-a-4 infraction occurs.

NOTE: An infraction of this rule may be penalized whether or not the ball is snapped and the penalty for any resultant offsides or contact foul other than unsportsmanlike or personal fouls by an opponent shall be canceled [S18 or S19 and S7].

b. **When the ball is snapped:**
   The offensive team must be in a formation that meets these requirements:
   1. At least seven players on their scrimmage line, not less than five of whom shall be numbered 50 through 79 (*Exception:* 1-4-2-b). The remaining players must be either on their scrimmage line or behind their backfield line, except as follows:
   2. One player may be between his scrimmage line and his backfield line if in a position to receive a hand-to-hand snap from between the snapper's legs. When in such position, that player may receive the snap himself or it may go directly to any player legally in the backfield [S19].
   3. The player on each side of and next to the snapper may lock legs with the snapper, but any other lineman of the team on offense must have both feet outside the outside foot of the player next to him when the ball is snapped [S19].
   4. All players must be in bounds and only the snapper may be encroaching on the neutral zone, but no part of his person may be beyond the neutral zone and his feet must be stationary behind the ball [S18 or S19].
   5. One offensive player may be in motion, but not in motion toward his opponents' goal line. If such player starts from his scrimmage line, he must be at least five yards behind that line when the ball is snapped. Other offensive players must be stationary in their positions without movement of the feet, body, head or arms [S20].

c. **After the ball is snapped:**
   1. No offensive lineman may receive a snap [S19].

PENALTY— For foul before ball is snapped: 5 yards from succeeding spot. For foul as or after ball is snapped: 5 yards from previous spot [S18, S19 or S20].

Defensive Team Requirements
ARTICLE 4. The defensive team requirements are as follows:

a. After the ball is ready for play and until it is snapped, no player on defense may touch the ball except when moved illegally as in 7-1-3-a-1 nor may any player contact an opponent or in any other way interfere with him [S7, S19]. An official shall sound his whistle immediately.
b. No defensive player may be in or beyond the neutral zone at the snap [S18].
c. No player of the team on defense shall use words or signals that disconcert opponents when they are preparing to put the ball in play. No player may call defensive signals that simulate the sound or cadence of (or otherwise interfere with) offensive starting signals. An official shall sound his whistle immediately [S7 and S19].

PENALTY— For foul before ball is snapped: 5 yards from succeeding spot. For fouls as or after ball is snapped: 5 yards from previous spot [S18 or S19].

Shift Plays
ARTICLE 5. a. If a snap is preceded by a huddle or shift, all players of the offensive team must come to an absolute stop and remain stationary in their positions, without movement of the feet, body, head or arms, for at least one full second before the ball is snapped.
b. It is not intended that Rule 7-1-3-a should prohibit smooth, rhythmical shifts if properly executed. A smooth, cadence shift or unhurried motion is not an infraction. However, it is the responsibility of an offensive player who moves before the snap to do so in a manner that in no way simulates the beginning of a play. After the ball is ready for play and all players are in scrimmage formation, no offensive player shall make a quick, jerky movement before the snap. Any such motion is an infraction of the rule. Although not intended to be all-inclusive, the following examples illustrate the type of movement prohibited before the snap:
   1. A lineman moving his foot, shoulder, arm, body or head in a quick, jerky motion in any direction.
   2. A center shifting or moving the ball, or moving his thumb or fingers, or flexing elbows, jerking head or dipping shoulders or buttocks.
   3. The quarterback "chucking" hands at center, flexing elbows under center or dropping shoulders quickly just before the snap.
   4. A player starting in motion before the snap simulating receiving the ball by "chucking" his hands toward the center or quarterback, or making any quick, jerky movement that simulates the beginning of a play.
   5. After an interior offensive lineman or a player numbered 50 through 79, who is on the line of scrimmage, has assumed a position with hand or hands on or near the ground (below the knee) he is restricted in movement until the ball is snapped (7-1-3-a-3).

   PENALTY—5 yards from previous spot [S7 and S20].

Handling the Ball Forward
ARTICLE 6. No player may hand the ball forward except during a scrimmage down as follows:
a. A Team A player who is behind his scrimmage line may hand the ball forward to a backfield teammate who is also behind that line.
b. A Team A player who is behind his scrimmage line may hand the ball forward to a teammate who was on his scrimmage line when the ball was snapped, provided that teammate left his line position by a movement of both feet that faced him toward his own end line and was at least one yard behind his scrimmage line when he received the ball.

PENALTY—5 yards from spot of foul also, loss of a down if by Team A before team possession changes during a scrimmage down [S35 and S9].

SECTION 2. Backward Pass and Fumble

During Live Ball
ARTICLE 1. a. A runner may hand or pass the ball backward at any time, except to throw the ball intentionally out of bounds to conserve time.

b. A snap is a backward pass; however, it may not go directly to a lineman of Team A.

PENALTY—5 yards from spot of foul also, loss of down if by Team A before team possession changes during a scrimmage down [S36 and S9].

Caught or Recovered
ARTICLE 2. A backward pass or fumble may be caught or recovered by any inbounds player (*Exception:* 7-2-1b):

a. If caught in flight in bounds, the ball continues in play unless the catch is made on or behind the opponent's goal line;
b. If recovered by the fumbling or passing team, the ball continues in play;
c. If recovered by the opponent of the fumbling or passing team, the ball becomes dead and belongs to his team where recovered;
d. If a backward pass or fumble is caught or recovered simultaneously by opposing players, the ball becomes dead and belongs to the team last in possession.

Out of Bounds
ARTICLE 3. When a backward pass or fumble goes out of bounds between the goal lines, the ball belongs to the passing or fumbling team at the out-of-bounds spot; if out of bounds behind a goal line, it is a touchback or a safety (*Exception:* 9-4-2).

SECTION 3. Forward Pass

Legal Forward Pass
ARTICLE 1. Team A may make one forward pass during each scrimmage down before team possession changes, provided the pass is thrown from a point in or behind the neutral zone.

Illegal Forward Pass
ARTICLE 2. A forward pass is illegal:

a. If thrown by Team A when the passer is beyond the neutral zone.
b. If thrown by Team B, or if thrown by Team A after team possession has changed during the down.
c. If it is the second forward pass by Team A during the same down.
d. If intentionally thrown into an area not occupied by an eligible Team A player to save loss of yardage or directly to the ground to conserve time.

PENALTY—5 yards from spot of foul also, loss of a down if by Team A before team possession changes during a scrimmage down [S35 or S36 and S9].

Eligibility to Touch Legal Pass
ARTICLE 3. Eligibility rules apply only when a legal forward pass is thrown. All Team B players are eligible to touch or catch a pass. When the ball is snapped, the following Team A players are eligible:
a. Each player who is in an end position on his scrimmage line and who is wearing a number other than 50 through 79.
b. Each player who is legally in his backfield wearing a number other than 50 through 79.
c. A player wearing a number other than 50 through 79, in position to receive a hand-to-hand snap from between the snapper's legs.

Eligibility Lost by Going Out of Bounds
ARTICLE 4. No eligible offensive player who goes out of bounds during a down shall touch a legal forward pass in the field of play or end zone until it has been touched by an opponent.
   Exception: This does not apply to an eligible offensive player who attempts to return in bounds immediately after being blocked or pushed out of bounds by an opponent.
PENALTY—Loss of down at previous spot [S31 and S9] .

Eligibility Regained
ARTICLE 5. When a Team B player touches a legal forward pass all players become eligible.

Completed Pass
ARTICLE 6. Any forward pass is completed when caught by a player of the passing team who is in bounds, and the ball continues in play unless the completion results in a touchdown or the pass has been caught simultaneously by opposing players. If a forward pass is caught simultaneously by opposing players in bounds, the ball becomes dead and belongs to the passing team.

Incompleted Pass
ARTICLE 7. a. Any forward pass is incomplete when the pass touches the ground or goes out of bounds. It is also incomplete when a player jumps and receives the pass but first lands on or outside a boundary line unless his forward progress has been stopped in the field of play (2-2-7-c).
b. When a legal forward pass is incomplete, the ball belongs to the passing team at the previous spot.
c. When an illegal forward pass is incomplete, the ball belongs to the passing team at the spot of the pass (*Exception:* If any illegal pass is thrown from the end zone, the offended team may accept a safety or decline the penalty and accept the result of the play.) (4-1-3-f).

Illegal Contact and Pass Interference
ARTICLE 8. a. During a down in which a legal forward pass crosses the neutral zone, illegal contact by Team A and Team B players is prohibited from the time the ball is snapped until it is touched by any player.
b. Offensive pass interference by a Team A player beyond the neutral zone during a legal forward pass play in which a forward pass crosses the neutral zone is contact that interferes with a Team B eligible player. It is the responsibility of the offensive player to avoid the opponents. It is not offensive pass interference if it is the type that occurs:

1. When, immediately following the snap, a Team A player charges and contacts an opponent at a point not more than one yard beyond the neutral zone and does not continue the contact beyond three yards.
2. When two or more eligible players are making a simultaneous and bona fide attempt to reach, catch or bat the pass. Eligible players of either team have equal rights to the ball.

c. Defensive pass interference is contact beyond the neutral zone by a Team B player whose intent to impede an eligible opponent is obvious and it could prevent the opponent the opportunity of receiving a catchable forward pass. When in question, a legal forward pass is catchable. Defensive pass interference occurs only after a forward pass is thrown. It is not defensive pass interference if it is the type that occurs (9-3-4-c, d and e):

1. When, immediately following the snap, opposing players charge and establish contact with opponents at a point that is within one yard beyond the neutral zone.
2. When two or more eligible players are making a simultaneous and bona fide attempt to reach, catch or bat the pass, eligible players of either team have equal rights to the ball.
3. When a Team B player legally contacts an opponent before the pass is thrown (see Rule 9-3-4-c and d).

PENALTY—Pass interference by Team A: 15 yards from previous spot plus loss of down [S33 and S9].
Pass interference by Team B: Team A's ball at spot of foul, first down. No penalty enforced from outside the two-yard line may place the ball inside the two-yard line.
If the previous spot was on or inside the two-yard line, first down halfway between the previous spot and the goal line [S33] (see Rule 10-2-3 Exception).

NOTE: When the ball is snapped between the Team B 17-yard line and the Team B two yard line and the spot of the foul is inside the two-yard line or in the end zone, the penalty shall place the ball at the two-yard line.

Contact Interference

ARTICLE 9. a. Either A or B may legally interfere with opponents behind the neutral zone.
b. Players of either team may legally interfere beyond the neutral zone after the pass has been touched.
c. Defensive players may legally contact opponents who have crossed the neutral zone if the opponents are not in a position to receive a catchable forward pass.
1. Those infractions that occur during a down when a forward pass crosses the neutral zone are pass interference only if the receiver had the opportunity to receive a catchable forward pass.
2. Those infractions that occur during a down when a forward pass does not cross the neutral zone are 9-3-4 infractions and are penalized from the previous spot.
d. Pass interference rules apply only during a down in which a legal forward pass crosses the neutral zone (A.R. 47) (2-19-3) (7-3-8-a and c).
e. Contact by B with an eligible receiver that involves unnecessary roughness that interferes with a catchable pass is penalized as pass interference, but fouls occurring less than 15 yards beyond the neutral zone may be penalized 15 yards as personal fouls from the previous spot. Rule 7-3-8 is specific about contact during a pass. However, if the interference involves an act that would ordinarily result in disqualification, the fouling player must leave the game.

59

f. Physical contact is required to establish interference.
g. Each player has territorial rights and incidental contact is ruled under "attempt to reach . . . the pass" in 7-3-8. If opponents who are beyond the line collide while moving toward the pass, a foul by one or both players is indicated only if intent to impede the opponent is obvious. It is pass interference by Team B only if a catchable forward pass is involved.
h. Pass interference rules do not apply after the pass has been touched anywhere in bounds by an in-bounds player. Players may tackle without waiting to determine possession and control, and players who are entitled to touch the pass may use his hand or arm to push opponents out of the way if there is a reasonable opportunity to reach the pass and if there is an actual attempt to reach it. If an opponent is fouled, the penalty is for the foul and not pass interference.
i. After the pass has been touched, any player may execute a legal block during the remaining flight of the pass.
j. Tackling or grasping a receiver or any other intentional contact before he touches the pass is evidence that the tackler is disregarding the ball and is therefore illegal.
k. Tackling or running into a receiver when a forward pass is obviously underthrown or overthrown is disregarding the ball and is illegal. This is not pass interference but a violation of 9-1-2-f and is penalized 15 yards from the previous spot.

Ineligibles Downfield

ARTICLE 10. No ineligible player shall be or have been beyond the neutral zone until a legal forward pass that crosses the neutral zone has been thrown.

Exceptions:
1. Immediately after the snap, offensive players may charge into opponents and drive them back no more than three yards from the neutral zone provided contact is established at a point not more than one yard beyond the neutral zone.
2. When contact that has driven an opponent no more than three yards from the neutral zone is lost by a player who was ineligible at the snap, he must remain stationary at that spot until the pass is thrown.

PENALTY—5 yards from previous spot plus loss of down [S37 and S9].

Illegal Touching

ARTICLE 11. No originally ineligible player while in bounds shall touch a legal forward pass until it has touched an opponent.

PENALTY—5 yards from previous spot plus loss of a down [S31 and S9].

RULE 8

Scoring

SECTION 1. Value of Scores

Scoring Plays
ARTICLE E. The point value of scoring plays shall be:

Touchdown .... 6 Points
Field Goal .... 3 Points
Safety (points awarded to opponents) .... 2 Points
Point after Touchdown (run or pass) .... 2 Points
Point after Touchdown (kick) .... 1 Point

SECTION 2. Touchdown

How Scored
ARTICLE 1. A touchdown shall be scored when a legal forward pass is completed or a fumble or backward pass is caught on or behind the opponents' goal line or when a player is legally in possession of the ball while any part of it is on, above or behind his opponents' goal line.

SECTION 3. Try

Opportunity to Score
ARTICLE 1. A try is an opportunity to score one or two additional points while the game clock is stopped and is a special interval in a game which, for purposes of penalty enforcement only, includes both a down and the "ready" period that precedes it.
a.   Opportunity shall be granted a team that has scored a touchdown.
b.   The try, which is a scrimmage down, begins when the ball is ready for play.

c. The snap may be from any point on or between the in-bounds lines on or behind the opponents' three-yard line and the ball may be relocated following a charged timeout to either team unless preceded by a Team A foul or offsetting penalties (8-3-3-a and 8-3-3-c-1).

d. The opportunity ends if:
    1. Team B gains possession of the ball or is entitled to possession after a foul;
    2. If a penalty against Team A involves loss of a down;
    3. If the accepted penalty results in a score.
    4. If it is obvious a scrimmage kick is unsuccessful.

How Scored
ARTICLE 2. The point or points shall be scored if the try results in what would be a touchdown, safety or field goal under rules governing play at other times.

Foul During Try for Point
ARTICLE 3. **a. Offsetting fouls:** The down shall be replayed if offsetting fouls occur. Any replay after offsetting penalties must be from the previous spot.

b. **Fouls by B on successful try:**
    1. Team A shall have the option of declining the score and repeating the try following enforcement, or accepting the score with enforcement of the penalty from the spot of the next kickoff.
    2. A replay after a penalty against Team B may be from any point between the in-bounds lines on the yard line where the penalty leaves the ball.

c. **Fouls by A on successful try:**
    1. After a foul by Team A, the ball shall be put in play at the spot where the penalty leaves it.

Next Play
ARTICLE 4. After a try the ball shall be put in play by a kickoff. The field captain of the team against which the touchdown was scored shall designate which team shall kick off.

SECTION 4. Field Goal

How Scored
ARTICLE 1. a. A field goal shall be scored for the kicking team if a drop kick or place kick passes over the crossbar between the uprights of the receiving team's goal before it touches a player of the kicking team or the ground. The kick shall be a scrimmage kick but may not be a free kick.

b. If a legal field goal attempt passes over the crossbar between the uprights and is grounded beyond the end lines or is blown back but does not return over the crossbar and is grounded anywhere, it shall score a field goal. The entire goal, crossbar, and uprights are treated as a **line** not a **plane** in determining forward progress of the ball.

Next Play
ARTICLE 2. a. After a field goal is scored the ball shall be put in play by a kickoff. The field captain of the team scored against shall designate which team shall kick off.

b. Following an unsuccessful field goal attempt that crosses the neutral zone, the ball, untouched by Team B beyond the neutral zone, will next be put in play at the previous spot. If the previous spot was between Team B's 20-yard line and goal line, the ball shall next be put in play at the 20-yard line. Otherwise, all rules pertaining to scrimmage kicks apply.

SECTION 5. Safety and Touchback

How Scored
ARTICLE 1. Touchback or safety.
a. It is a touchback:
   1. When the ball is out of bounds behind a goal line (except from an incompleted forward pass). If the attacking team is responsible for the ball being behind that goal line (*Exception:* 8-4-2-b).
   2. When the ball becomes dead in possession of a player on, above or behind his own goal line and the attacking team is responsible for the ball being on, above or behind that goal line.
b. It is a safety:
   1. When the ball becomes dead in the possession of a player on, above or behind his own goal line and the defending team is responsible for the ball being on, above or behind the goal line.
   2. When an accepted penalty for a foul or an illegal forward pass leaves the ball on or behind the offending team's goal line.

   Exception: When a Team B player intercepts a forward pass or catches a scrimmage or free kick between his five-yard line and the goal line and his original momentum carries him into the end zone where the ball is declared dead in his team's possession or he goes out of bounds in the end zone, the ball belongs to Team B at the spot where the pass was intercepted or the kick caught.

Responsibility
ARTICLE 2. The team responsible for the ball being on, above or behind a goal line is the team whose player carries the ball or imparts an impetus to it that forces it on, above or across that goal line; or is responsible for a loose ball being on, above or behind the goal line.

Initial Impetus
ARTICLE 3. The impetus imparted by a player who kicks, passes, snaps or fumbles the ball shall be considered responsible for the ball's progress in any direction even though its course is deflected or reversed after striking the ground or after touching a player of either team. However, the initial impetus is considered expended and the responsibility for the progress of the ball is charged to a player: if he kicks a ball not in player possession or bats a loose ball after it strikes the ground; or if the ball comes to rest and he gives it new impetus by any contact with it.

Resulting From Foul
ARTICLE 4. If the penalty for a foul committed when the ball is loose leaves the ball behind the offender's goal line, it is a safety.

Kick After Safety
ARTICLE 5. When a safety is scored the ball belongs to the defending team at its own 20-yard line and that team shall put the ball in play between the in-bounds lines by a free kick that may be a punt, drop kick or place kick.

Snap After Touchback
ARTICLE 6. After a touchback is declared the ball shall belong to the defending team at its own 20-yard line and that team shall put the ball in play between the in-bounds lines by snap.

RULE 9

Conduct of Players and Others Subject to Rules

SECTION 1. Contact and Interference Fouls

Personal Fouls
ARTICLE 1. During the game and between periods, all flagrant fouls require disqualification. Team B disqualification fouls may require first downs if not in conflict with other rules.

Player Restrictions
ARTICLE 2. No person subject to the rules shall commit a personal foul during the game or between the periods. Any act prohibited hereunder or any other act of unnecessary roughness is a personal foul.

a. No player shall strike an opponent with the knee, or strike an opponent's head, neck or face or any part of the body with an extended forearm, elbow, locked hands, palm, fist or the heel, back or side of the open hand or gouge an opponent during the game or between the periods.

b. No player shall strike an opponent with his foot or any part of his leg that is below the knee.

c. There shall be no *tripping*.

d. There shall be no *clipping*.

   Exception: During a scrimmage down, only offensive players on the line of scrimmage at the snap within a rectangular area centered on the middle lineman of the offensive formation and extending five yards laterally in each direction and three yards longitudinally in each direction, may legally clip in the rectangular area. A player on the line of scrimmage within the legal clipping zone may not leave the zone and return and legally clip. The legal clipping zone exists until the ball is in player possession outside the legal clipping zone or has been muffed or fumbled outside the legal clipping zone.

e. Blocking below the waist is permitted except as follows:

1. Offensive players at the snap positioned more than seven yards in any direction from the middle lineman of the offensive formation or in motion toward the ball at the snap are prohibited from blocking below the waist toward the ball until the ball has advanced beyond the neutral zone. The following formation sets are legal and the players are not restricted by 9-1-2-e when blocking toward the ball:
   (a) An offensive end positioned less than two yards from the legal clipping zone.
   (b) A wingback positioned one yard to the outside of an end who is flexed no more than one yard from the legal clipping zone.
   (c) A wingback positioned no more than one yard outside the legal clipping zone and inside an end who is one yard outside the wingback.
2. During a scrimmage down, defensive players are prohibited from blocking an eligible Team A receiver below the waist beyond the legal clipping zone extended to the sideline unless attempting to get at the ball or runner. A Team A receiver remains eligible until a legal forward pass is no longer possible by rule.
3. During a down in which there is a free kick or scrimmage kick from a scrimmage kick formation, all players are prohibited from blocking below the waist except against the runner.
4. After any change of possession all players are prohibited from blocking below the waist except against the runner.
5. A Team A player behind the neutral zone and in position to receive a backward pass shall not be blocked below the waist.

f. No player shall tackle or run into a receiver when a forward pass to him is obviously not catchable. This is not pass interference.
g. There shall be no *piling* on, falling on, or throwing the body on an opponent after the ball becomes dead.
h. No opponent shall tackle or block the runner *when he is clearly out of bounds* or throw him to the ground after the ball becomes dead.
i. There shall be no *hurdling*.
j. No player shall run into or *throw himself* against an opponent obviously out of the play either before or after the ball is dead.
k. No player shall grasp the face mask or any helmet opening of an opponent. The open hand may be legally used on the mask.

PENALTY— Defensive team 5 yards incidental grasping, 15 yards and first down against Team B for twisting, turning or pulling. Offensive team 15 yards. All dead-ball fouls 15 yards. Flagrant offenders shall be disqualified [S45].

l. No player shall intentionally use his helmet to butt or ram an opponent.
m. There shall be no *spearing*.
n. No player shall intentionally strike a runner with the crown or the top of his helmet.
o. No defensive player shall charge into a passer when it is obvious the ball has been thrown.
p. The kicker of a free kick may not be blocked until he has advanced five yards beyond his restraining line or the kick has touched a player, an official or the ground.
q. There shall be no chop blocking.

PENALTY— 15 yards and a first down for 9-1-2-a, b, g, h, j, l, m, n and o if Team B fouls and the first down is not in conflict with other rules [S34, S38, S39, S40, S41, S45 or S46]. Flagrant offenders shall be disqualified [S47].

Roughing or Running into Kicker or Holder

ARTICLE 3. a. When it is obvious that a scrimmage kick will be made, no opponent shall run into or rough the kicker or the holder of a place kick.

1. Roughing is a personal foul that endangers the kicker or holder.
2. Running into the kicker or holder is a foul that occurs when the kicker or holder are displaced from their kicking or holding positions but are not roughed.
3. Incidental contact with a kicker or holder is not a foul.
4. The kicker and holder must be protected from injury but contact that occurs when or after a scrimmage kick has been touched is not roughing or running into the kicker.
5. The kicker of a scrimmage kick loses protection as a kicker when he has had a reasonable time to regain his balance.

PENALTY—5 yards previous spot for running into kicker or holder. 15 yards previous spot and also first down for roughing kicker or holder [S30]. Flagrant offenders shall be disqualified [S47].

b. A kicker or holder simulating being roughed or run into by a defensive player commits an unfair act.

PENALTY—15 yards previous spot [S27].

Illegal Interference

ARTICLE 4. a. No substitute, coach, authorized attendant or any person subject to the rules other than a player or official, may interfere in any way with the ball or a player while the ball is in play.

b. Participation by 12 or more players is illegal participation.

PENALTY—15 yards from the spot most advantageous to the offended team. The referee may enforce any penalty he considers equitable, including awarding a score [S27, S28, S47].

Game Administration Interference

ARTICLE 5. a. While the ball is in play, coaches, substitutes and authorized attendants in the team area may not be between the sidelines and coaching line.

b. The procedure for enforcement of 9-1-5-a is as follows:

1. The head coach is informed by a game official that he is receiving a first or second warning because the area between the sideline and coaching line has been violated by coaches, players or persons authorized in the team area.
2. The official will record the time and period of each warning.
3. After a second warning, the official will notify the head coach that he has had two warnings and that the next infraction will result in a five-yard penalty.
4. After a five-yard penalty, the official will notify the head coach that he has had two warnings and a five-yard penalty and will receive a 15-yard penalty for the next infraction.
5. Warnings shall be given only when the clock is stopped.

PENALTY—5 yards after two official warnings from a game official and 15 yards for each additional foul. Penalize as a dead-ball foul [S29].

c. Crowd noise, including bands and other persons subject to the rules, that prohibits a team from hearing its signals is an unfair act (3-3-3-f-4) **VIOLATION 3-3-6 and 3-4-2-b. [S3 or S21].**

SECTION 2. Noncontact Fouls

Unsportsmanlike Acts
ARTICLE 1. There shall be no unsportsmanlike conduct or any act that interferes with orderly game administration on the part of players, substitutes, coaches, authorized attendants or any other persons subject to the rules, either during the game or between periods.

a. Specifically prohibited acts and conduct include:
1. No player, substitute, coach, authorized attendant or other persons subject to the rules shall use abusive or insulting language to players or officials or indulge in any conduct that might incite players or spectators against officials.
2. If a player is injured, attendants may come in bounds to attend him but they must obtain recognition from an official.
3. No person subject to the rules, except players, officials and eligible substitutes, shall be on the field of play or end zones during any period without permission from the referee (*Exception:* 3-3-5).
4. After a score or any other play the player in possession must immediately return the ball to an official or leave it near the dead-ball spot. This prohibits:
   a. Taking a ball off the field of play or end zones.
   b. Kicking or throwing the ball any distance that requires an official to retrieve it.
   e. Throwing the ball high into the air.
   f. Any other unsportsmanlike act or actions that delay the game.
5. No player or substitute shall use language, gestures or engage in acts that provoke ill will including:
   a. Swinging a hand or arm and missing an opponent or kicking and missing an opponent.
   b. Pointing the ball at an opponent.
   c. Baiting an opponent verbally.
   d. Inciting an opponent in any other way.
6. No substitutes may enter the field of play or end zones for purposes other than replacing a player. This includes demonstrations after any play.

PENALTY—15 yards [S7 and S27]. Succeeding spot. Penalize as a dead-ball foul. Flagrant offenders, if players or substitutes, shall be disqualified [S47].

b. Other prohibited acts include:
1. During the game, coaches, substitutes and authorized attendants in the team area shall not be on the field of play or outside the 25- or 30-yard lines without permission from the referee unless legally entering or leaving the field (*Exception:* 3-3-8-c).
2. No disqualified player shall enter the field.

PENALTY—15 yards [S7, S27]. Succeeding spot. Penalize as a dead-ball foul. Flagrant offenders, if players or substitutes, shall be disqualified [S47].

Unfair Tactics
ARTICLE 2. a. No player shall conceal the ball beneath his clothing or substitute any other article for the ball.
b. No simulated replacements or substitutions may be used to confuse opponents.

PENALTY—15 yards [S27]. Enforcement spot (10-2-2). Penalize as a live-ball foul. Flagrant offenders shall be disqualified [S47].

Unfair Acts
ARTICLE 3. a. The referee may enforce any penalty he considers equitable, including awarding a score:
  1. If a team refuses to play within two minutes after ordered to do so by the referee.
  2. If a team repeatedly commits fouls that can be penalized only by halving the distance to its goal line.

  The referee shall, after one warning, forfeit the game to the opponents for 9-2-3-a-1 & 2 infractions.

b. The referee may enforce any penalty he considers equitable, including awarding a score, if an obviously unfair act not specifically covered by the rules occurs during the game.

SECTION 3. Blocking, Use of Hand and Arm

Who May Block
ARTICLE 1. Players of either team may block opponents provided it is not forward pass interference with opportunity to catch a kick, or a personal foul.

Interfering for or Helping the Runner
ARTICLE 2. a. The runner or passer may use his hand or arm to ward off or push opponents.
b. The runner shall not grasp a teammate, and no other player of his team shall grasp, push, lift or charge into him to assist him in forward progress.
c. Teammates of the runner or passer may interfere for him by blocking but shall not use interlocked interference by grasping or encircling one another in any manner while contacting an opponent.

PENALTY—5 yards [S44].

Use of Hand or Arm by Offense
ARTICLE 3. a. A teammate of a runner or a passer may legally block with his shoulders, hands, outer surface of his arms or any other part of his body under the following provisions.
  1. The hand(s) shall be:
    a. In advance of the elbow.
    b. Inside the frame of the blocker's body.
    c. Inside the frame of the opponent's body (*Exception:* When the opponent turns his back to the blocker).
    d. At or below the shoulder(s) of the blocker and the opponent.
  2. The hand(s) shall be open with the palm(s) facing the frame of the opponent or closed or cupped with the palms not facing the opponent.

PENALTY—5 yards basic spot. 5 yards previous spot when the foul is behind the neutral zone [S43].

b. Holding or illegal obstruction by a teammate of the runner or passer applies to 9-3-3-a:
  1. The hand(s) and arm(s) shall not be used to grasp, pull or encircle in any way that illegally impedes or illegally obstructs an opponent.

2. The hand(s) or arm(s) shall not be used to hook, lock, clamp or otherwise illegally impede or illlegally obstruct an opponent.

PENALTY— 10 yards basic spot. 10 yards previous spot when the foul is behind the neutral zone [S42].

c. The following acts by a teammate of the runner or passer are illegal:
 1. The hand(s) and arm(s) shall not be used to deliver a blow.
 2. During no block shall the hands be locked.

PENALTY—15 yards basic spot [S38]. Disqualification if flagrant [S47].

d. A crab or cross-body block is legal if there is no illegal contact with the hand(s) or arm(s).

 PENALTY—5 yards [S43].

e. A player on the kicking team may:
 1. During a scrimmage kick play, use his hand(s) and/or arm(s) to ward off an opponent attempting to block him when he is beyond the neutral zone.
 2. During a free kick play, use his hand(s) and/or arm(s) to ward off an opponent who is attempting to block him.
 3. During a scrimmage kick play when he is eligible to touch the ball, legally use his hand(s) and/or arm(s) to push an opponent in an attempt to reach a loose ball.
 4. During a free kick play when he is eligible to touch the ball, legally use his hand(s) and/or arm(s) to push an opponent obstructing his attempt to reach a loose ball.
f. A player of the passing team may legally use his hand(s) and/or arm(s) to ward off or push an opponent in an attempt to reach a loose ball after a legal forward pass has been touched by any player.

Use of Hands or Arms by Defense
ARTICLE 4. a. Defensive players may use hands and arms to push, pull, grasp, ward off or lift offensive players when attempting to reach the runner.
b. Defensive players may not use hands and arms to tackle, hold or otherwise illegally obstruct an opponent other than a runner.

PENALTY—10 yards basic spot [S42].

c. Defensive players may use hands and arms to push, pull, grasp, ward off or lift offensive players obviously attempting to block them. Defensive players may ward off or push an eligible pass receiver until that player occupies the same yard line as the defender. Continuous contact is illegal or the opponent could possibly block him (7-3-8-c).

PENALTY—5 yards basic spot [S43].

d. When no attempt is being made to get at the ball or the runner, defensive players must comply with 9-3-3-a, b, c. (*Exception:* Pulling an offensive player out of the way to give a teammate the opportunity to block a kick or reach a runner is defensive holding only if the defensive man hangs on, or pulls the opponent to the ground with him.)

PENALTY—5, 10 or 15 yards basic spot [S43, S42 or S38].

e. When a legal forward pass crosses the neutral zone during a forward pass play and a contact foul that is not pass interference is committed, the enforcement spot is the previous spot. This includes Rule 9-3-4-c.

PENALTY—5, 10 or 15 yards plus first down if foul occurred against an eligible receiver before the ball was thrown [S43, S42 or S38].

f. A defensive player may legally use his hand or arm to ward off or push an opponent in an attempt to reach a loose ball:
1. During a backward pass, fumble or kick that he is eligible to touch.
2. During any forward pass that crossed the neutral zone and has been touched by any player.

Player Restrictions
ARTICLE 5. a. No player may position himself with his feet on the back or shoulders of a teammate prior to the snap.

PENALTY—Dead-ball foul 15 yards [S27].

b. No defensive player, in an attempt to block a kick, may:
1. Step, jump or stand on a teammate or an opponent;
2. Place a hand(s) on a teammate to get leverage for additional height;
3. Be picked up by a teammate.

PENALTY—15 yards basic spot [S27].

When Ball is Loose
ARTICLE 6. When the ball is loose, no player shall grasp, pull or tackle an opponent or commit a personal foul.

PENALTY—10 or 15 yards from the basic or previous spot (10-2-2-c, d, e, f) [S38 or S42].

SECTION 4. Batting and Kicking

Batting a Loose Ball
ARTICLE 1. a. While a pass is in flight, any player eligible to touch the ball may bat it in any direction.
b. Any player may block or partially block a scrimmage kick in the field of play or the end zone.
c. No player shall bat other loose balls forward in the field of play or in any direction if they are in the end zone.

PENALTY—15 yards from the basic or previous spot (10-2-2-c, d, e, f) [S31].

Batting a Backward Pass
ARTICLE 2. A backward pass in flight shall not be batted forward by the passing team in an attempt to gain yardage.

PENALTY—15 yards from the basic or previous spot (10-2-2-c) [S31].

Batting Ball in Possession
ARTICLE 3. A ball in player possession may not be batted by a player of that team.

PENALTY—15 yards from the basic or previous spot (10-2-2-c) [S31].

Illegally Kicking Ball

ARTICLE 4. A player shall not kick a loose ball, a forward pass or a ball being held for a place kick by an opponent. These illegal acts do not change the status of the loose ball or forward pass; but if the player holding the ball for a place kick loses possession during a scrimmage down, it is a fumble and a loose ball; if during a free kick, the ball remains dead.

PENALTY— 15 yards from the basic or previous spot, also loss of down (10-2-2-c, d, e, f) [S9 and S31].

RULE 10

Penalty Enforcement

SECTION 1. Penalties Completed

How and When Completed
ARTICLE 1. A penalty is completed when it is accepted, declined, canceled according to rule, or when the most advantageous choice is obvious to the referee. Any penalty may be declined, but a disqualified player must leave the game. When a foul is committed at a time other than following a touchdown and before the ball is ready for play on a try, the penalty shall be completed before the ball is declared ready for play for any ensuing down (*Exception:* 10-2-2-g-2 Touchdown).

Simultaneous with Snap
ARTICLE 2. A foul that occurs simultaneously with a snap or free kick is considered as occurring during that down.

Live-Ball Fouls by the Same Team
ARTICLE 3. When two or more live-ball fouls by the same team are reported to the referee, the referee shall explain the alternative penalties to the field captain of the offended team who may then elect only one of these penalties (*Exception:* When a foul (or fouls) for unsportsmanlike conduct (noncontact fouls) occurs, the penalty (or penalties) is administered from the succeeding spot as established by the acceptance or declination of the penalty for any other foul).

Offsetting Fouls
ARTICLE 4. If live-ball fouls by both teams are reported to the referee, each such foul is an offsetting foul and the penalties cancel each other and the down is replayed.
Exceptions:
1. When there is a change of team possession during a down or at the end of a down by rule, the team last gaining possession may decline offsetting fouls and thereby retain possession after completion of the penalty for its infraction if it had not fouled prior to its gaining possession.
2. When Team B's foul is postscrimmage kick enforcement, Team B may decline offsetting fouls and accept postscrimmage kick enforcement.
3. When a live-ball foul is administered as a dead-ball foul, it does not offset and is enforced in order of occurrence.

Dead-Ball Fouls
ARTICLE 5. Penalties for dead-ball fouls are administered separately and in order of occurrence.

Exception: When dead-ball fouls by both teams are reported and the order of occurrence cannot be determined, the fouls cancel, the number or type of down established before the fouls occurred is unaffected, and the penalties are disregarded, except that any disqualified player must leave the game (10-2-2-a) (5-2-6).

Live-Ball—Dead-Ball Fouls
ARTICLE 6. When a live-ball foul by one team is followed by one or more dead-ball fouls (or live-ball fouls penalized as dead-ball fouls) by an opponent or by the same team, the penalties are administered separately and in the order of occurrence.

Interval Fouls
ARTICLE 7. Fouls that occur in different down intervals between the scoring of a touchdown and the succeeding kickoff shall be enforced in the order of their occurrences.

SECTION 2. Enforcement Procedures

Spots
ARTICLE 1. The enforcement spots are: the previous spot, the spot of the foul, the succeeding spot, the spot where the kick ends and the spot where the run ends.

Procedures
ARTICLE 2. When no enforcement spot is specified in a rule penalty, the following procedures apply:
a.   Dead ball — The enforcement spot for a foul committed when the ball is dead is the succeeding spot.
b.   Snap or free kick — The enforcement spot for fouls occurring simultaneously with a snap or free kick is the previous spot.
c.   Running plays — The basic enforcement spots for fouls that occur during running plays in the field of play or end zone are as follows:
   1. When the run ends beyond the neutral zone, the basic enforcement spot is the end of the related run (2-25-10-a) (*Exception:* 9-3-3-a and b).
   2. When the run ends behind the neutral zone before a change of team possession, the basic enforcement spot is the previous spot (2-25-10-b) (*Exception:* 9-3-3-a and b).
   3. When there is no neutral zone, the basic enforcement spot is the end of the related run (2-25-10-c).
d.   Pass plays — The basic enforcement spot for fouls during a legal forward pass play is the previous spot. (*Exceptions:* Team B pass interference spot fouls and 9-3-3-a, b fouls.)
e.   Kick plays — The basic enforcement spot for fouls that occur during a legal free or scrimmage kick play before possession is gained or regained or the ball is declared dead by rule is the previous spot.

   Exceptions:
   1. Interference with the opportunity to make a catch—spot foul (6-4-1).
   2. Team A, during a scrimmage kick, bats a loose ball behind Team B's goal line — a live-ball foul and a touchback.

3. A block or foul after a valid, invalid or illegal signal for a fair catch by a Team B player who signaled for a fair catch during a free kick and had not touched the ball —spot foul (6-5-4).
4. Illegal fair catch signal during a free kick —spot foul (6-5-3).
5. Postscrimmage kick enforcement.
   The basic enforcement spot for Team B fouls during scrimmage kick plays, other than tries, that cross the neutral zone and occur beyond the legal clipping zone extended to the sideline and prior to player possession, is the spot where the kick ends (see Rule 2-25-9).
6. The enforcement spot for illegal participation during a free or scrimmage kick plays is the spot most advantageous to the offended team (see Rule 9-1-4).
7. 9-3-3-a and b fouls behind the neutral zone.

f. Behind the goal line.
1. The enforcement spot is the goal line for fouls by the opponents of the team in possession after a change of team possession in the field of play when the run ends behind the goal line. Safety if no foul occurred (*Exception:* 8-5-1).
2. The basic enforcement spot is the 20-yard line for fouls that occur after a change of team possession in the end zone and the ball remains in the end zone where it is declared dead. These are live-ball fouls. Touchback if no foul occurred.

g. Interval fouls—Succeeding kickoff.
1. When a foul occurs after a touchdown and before the ball is ready for play for the try, the enforcement is at the spot of the succeeding kickoff.
2. Distance penalties for fouls by opponents of the team in possession during a down that ends in a touchdown, a field goal or a successful try are penalized at the succeeding kickoff. All defensive pass interference fouls are penalized 15 yards from the succeeding spot. However, the field goal or the successful try (8-3-3) may be declined and the penalty enforced according to rule (*Exception:* 10-2-2-e-5).
3. Fouls that occur in different down intervals between the scoring of a touchdown and the succeeding kickoff shall be enforced in the order of their occurrence.
4. Distance penalties for fouls by the receiving team may not extend the receiving team's restraining line behind their five-yard line. Fouls that place the restraining line of the receiving team behind their five-yard line are enforced from the succeeding spot.

Half-distance enforcement procedures
ARTICLE 3. No distance penalty shall exceed half the distance from the enforcement spot to the offending team's goal line. (*Exception:* Defensive pass interference penalties other than those from the two-yard line or closer to the goal line.)

Summary of Penalties

OFFICIALS' SIGNALS [SEE PAGES 76-77], THE NUMBERS REFER TO
NUMBERED ILLUSTRATIONS: R, RULE; S, SECTION; A, ARTICLE

LOSS OF A DOWN

Index No.		O	R	S	A
1	Illegally handing ball forward [also loss of 5 yards]	35*	7	1	6
2	Intentionally throwing backward pass out of bounds [also loss of 5 yards]	36*	7	2	1
3	Illegal forward pass by Team A [also loss of 5 yards]	35*	7	3	2
4	Intentionally grounding forward pass [also loss of 5 yards]	36*	7	3	2
5	Forward pass illegally touched by player out of bounds	31*	7	3	4
6	Offensive pass interference [also loss of 15 yards]	33*	7	3	8
7	Ineligible receiver downfield [also loss of 5 yards]	37*	7	3	10
8	Forward pass illegally touched [also loss of 5 yards]	31*	7	3	11
9	Illegally kicking ball [also loss of 15 yards]	31*	9	4	3
10	Illegal Player, too many Americans [also loss of 15 yards]	22	3	5	2

LOSS OF 5 YARDS

		O	R	S	A
11	Improper numbering	23	1	4	2
12	Timeout charged after three expended	21	3	4	2
13	Illegal delay of the game	21	3	4	2
14	Crawling	21	3	4	2
15	Unfair tactics	21	3	4	3
16	Excess substitutes	22	3	5	2
17	Substitution rules infractions	22	3	5	2
18	Putting ball in play before declared ready for play	19	4	1	4
19	Exceeding 25-second count	21	4	1	5
20	Infraction of free kick formation	18, 19	6	1	2
21	Player out of bounds when ball free kicked	19	6	1	2
22	Free kick out of bounds	19	6	2	1
23	Illegal kick	31	6	3	10
24	Non-contact interference with opportunity to catch a kick	33	6	4	1
25	Taking more than two steps after fair catch	21	6	5	2
26	Illegal snap	19	7	1	1
27	Snapper's position and ball adjustment	19	7	1	3
28	Team A not within 15 yards after ready for play	19	7	1	3
29	False start or simulating start of a play	19	7	1	3
30	Interference with opponents or ball	19	7	1	3
31	Infraction of scrimmage formation	19	7	1	3

*Also Signal 9

32	Encroachment (offense) at snap [offside]	18	7	1	3
33	Player out of bounds when ball is snapped	19	7	1	3
34	Offensive player illegally in motion at the snap	20	7	1	3
35	Player on scrimmage line receiving snap	19	7	1	3
36	Defensive disconcerting signals	19	7	1	4
37	Failure to pause full second in shift play	20	7	1	5
38	Illegally handing ball forward [also loss of down if by Team A]	35*	7	1	6
39	Intentionally throwing backward pass out of bounds [also loss of down if by Team A]	36*	7	2	1
41	Illegal forward pass [also loss of down if by Team A] ..	35*	7	3	2
41	Intentionally grounding forward pass [also loss of down]	36*	7	3	2
42	Ineligible receiver downfield [also loss of down]	37*	7	3	9
43	Forward pass illegally touched [also loss of down]	31*	7	3	10
44	Defensive grasping facemask or helmet opening of opponent [also 15 yards]	45	9	1	2
45	Running into kicker or holder	30	9	1	3
46	Sideline-restraining line infraction [also 15 yards]	29	9	1	5
47	Interlocked interference or helping runner	44	9	3	2
48	Illegal use of hands (offense)	43	9	3	3
49	Illegal use of hands (defense)	43	9	3	4
50	Team A player illegally touching free kick	19	6	1	2
51	Offside (defense)	18	7	1	4

LOSS OF 10 YARDS

52	Home team delay	21	3	4	1
53	Holding or obstruction (offense)	42	9	3	3
54	Holding or obstruction (defense)	42	9	3	4
55	Holding or obstruction (loose ball)	42	9	3	6

LOSS OF 15 YARDS

56	Illegally batting a backward pass	31	9	4	1 & 2
57	Batting ball in possession by player in possession	31	9	4	3
58	Illegal signal devices, also disqualification	27	1	4	7
59	Team not ready to play at start of either half	21	3	4	1
60	Contact interference with opportunity to catch a kick [also 5 yards for noncontact foul]	33	6	4	1
61	Illegal signal for fair catch	32	6	5	3
62	Illegal block by fair catch signaller	40	6	5	4
63	Tackling or blocking fair catcher	38	6	5	5
64	Offensive pass interference [also loss of down]	33*	7	3	8
65	Defensive pass interference [also automatic first down]	33	7	3	8
66	Striking, kicking, kneeing, elbowing, etc. [first down] ..	38	9	1	2

*Also Signal 9

67	Meeting with knee, striking with open hand, etc. [first down]	38	9	1	2
68	Tripping	46	9	1	2
69	Clipping	39	9	1	2
70	Piling on [first down]	38	9	1	2
71	Tackling out of bounds [first down]	38	9	1	2
72	Hurdling	38	9	1	2
73	Grasping face mask or helmet or opponent [first down] [also 5 yards]	45	9	1	2
74	Offensive grasping of facemask or helmet opening of opponent	45	9	1	2
75	Butting or ramming with helmet [first down]	38	9	1	2
76	Roughing the passer [first down]	34	9	1	2
77	Top of helmet striking [first down]	38	9	1	2
78	Spearing [first down]	38	9	1	2
79	Chop Block	41	9	1	2
80	Simulating roughed or run into	27	9	1	3
81	Roughing the kicker or holder [first down]	30	9	1	3
82	Substitute interferes	27*	9	1	4
83	Illegal participation	28	9	1	4
84	Blocking below the waist	40	9	1	2
85	Abusive or insulting language	27	9	2	1
86	Persons illegally on the field	27	9	2	1
87	Player not returning ball to official	27	9	2	1
88	Engendering ill will	27	9	2	1
89	Unsportsmanlike conduct	27	9	2	1
90	Persons leave team area	27	9	2	1
91	Concealing the ball	27	9	2	2
92	Illegal return of disqualified player	27	9	2	1
93	Defensive restrictions	27	9	3	5
94	Illegally batting loose ball	31	9	4	1
95	Illegally kicking ball	31	9	4	4
96	Running into opponent out of play [first down]	38	9	1	2
97	Illegal substitution: too many Americans [also loss of down]	22	3	5	2

LOSS OF HALF DISTANCE TO GOAL LINE

98	If distance penalty exceeds half the distance except pass interference	—	10	2	1

OFFENDED TEAM'S BALL AT SPOT OF FOUL

99	Defensive pass interference [if not 15-yard penalty]	33	7	3	8

CHARGED TIMEOUT

100	Not wearing mandatory equipment	23	1	4	4
101	Wearing illegal equipment	23	1	4	5
102	Coaches' conference	21	3	3	4
103	Game interference (crowd noise)	21	9	1	5

*Also Signal 9

VIOLATION

| 104 | Illegal touching of free kick by kicking team | 31 | 6 | 3 | 2 |
| 105 | Illegal touching of scrimmage kick | 31 | 6 | 3 | 2 |

AUTOMATIC FIRST DOWNS

106	Defensive pass interference	33	7	3	8
107	Striking, kicking, kneeing, elbowing, etc.	38	9	1	2
108	Meeting with knee, striking with open hand etc.	38	9	1	2
109	Tackling out of bounds	38	9	1	2
110	Face mask defense (15 yards)	38	9	1	2
111	Butting or ramming with helmet	38	9	1	2
112	Spearing	38	9	1	2
113	Running into an opponent out of play	38	9	1	2
114	Top of helmet striking	38	9	1	2
115	Roughing the passer	38	9	1	2
116	Roughing the kicker or holder	30	9	1	3
117	Illegal use of hands (defense)**	43	9	3	4
118	Holding or obstruction (defense)**	43	9	3	4

*Also Signal 9
**Only under Rule 9-3-4-e

Officials' Signals

NOTE: Signals numbered 17, 25 and 26 are for future expansion.

1   Ball ready for play

2   Start clock

3   Time-out
     Discretionary or injury time-out
     (follow by tapping hands on
     chest)

4   TV or radio time-out

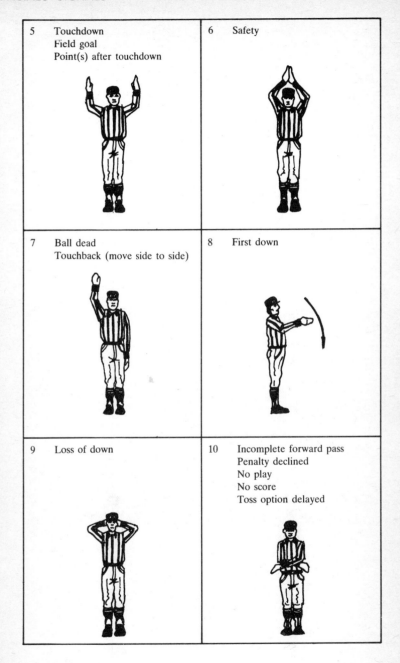

5 Touchdown Field goal Point(s) after touchdown	6 Safety
7 Ball dead Touchback (move side to side)	8 First down
9 Loss of down	10 Incomplete forward pass Penalty declined No play No score Toss option delayed

11 Legal touching of forward pass or scrimmage kick	12 Inadvertent whistle (face press box)
13 Disregard flag	14 End of period
15 Sideline warning	16 First touching Illegal touching

18 Encroachment Offside	19 Illegal procedure False start Illegal position
20 Illegal motion Illegal shift	21 Delay of game
22 Substitution infraction	23 Failure to wear required equipment

24 Illegal helmet contact	27 Unsportsmanlike conduct Noncontact foul
28 Illegal participation	29 Sideline interference
30 Running into or roughing kicker or holder	31 Ball illegally kicked, batted or touched

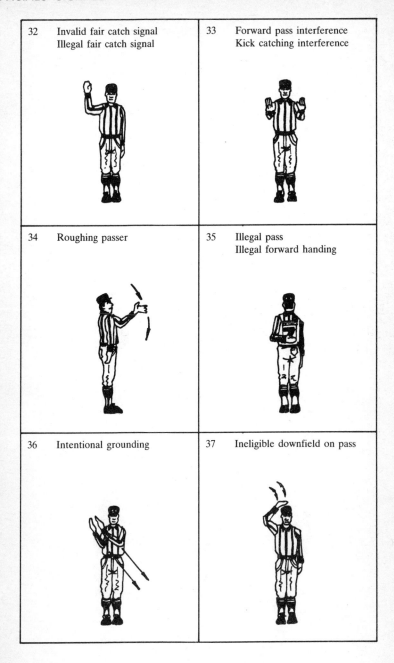

32   Invalid fair catch signal
       Illegal fair catch signal

33   Forward pass interference
       Kick catching interference

34   Roughing passer

35   Illegal pass
       Illegal forward handing

36   Intentional grounding

37   Ineligible downfield on pass

38   Personal foul

39   Clipping

40   Blocking below waist
       Illegal block

41   Chop block

42   Holding or obstructing

43   Illegal use of hands or arms

44 Helping runner Interlocked interference	45 Grasping face mask or helmet opening
46 Tripping	47 Player disqualification

The Officials:
Jurisdiction & Duties

General

The officials are jointly responsible for the enforcement of all rules and must cooperate closely in facilitating the orderly conduct of the game.

The referee must carry a whistle and sound it to indicate that the ball is ready for play during a timeout, that it has become dead or that he has suspended play. Other officials shall also carry whistles.

Each official must carry a marker and drop it whenever he calls a foul.

Each official must know and use arm signals, hereinafter prescribed, to indicate the fouls he calls or to indicate other rulings he makes.

Whenever a live ball or the runner goes out of bounds, the nearest official must signal "timeout" immediately and mark the out-of-bounds spot. The other officials must repeat that "timeout" signal at once.

If an official declares a foul during a down, he shall mark the spot, then report the foul to the referee when the ball becomes dead. A foul declared between successive downs shall be reported to the referee immediately. Upon request of the field captain the offending player shall be identified.

The nearest official shall report the position or number of the offending player to the offending player's coach.

Referee

The referee has general oversight and control of the game. He is sole authority for the score, sole judge of forfeiture of the game by rule and his decisions upon all rules and other matters pertaining to the game are final.

Whenever play is suspended by the referee he shall complete any penalty that may have been incurred; spot the ball where play is to resume; announce team possession for the next down; and indicate, by use of prescribed signal, that the ball is ready for play and start the clock.

The referee must see that the ball is put in play and declared dead according to rule, and he has final authority over the ball's position and progress.

Prior to the beginning of a game, the referee must test and select the game ball or balls. He must also inspect the entire field and report any irregularities to the field captains of each team and all officials.

If the referee orders the ball changed between downs, he may use an assistant on each sideline to expedite the exchanges.

After each timeout and before declaring the ball ready for play, the referee must make sure that both teams and all officials are ready.

Unless the most advantageous choice is obvious, the referee shall explain to the field captain any option or alternatives to which he may be entitled and then proceed in accordance with the choice first expressed by that field captain.

The referee must instantly signal "timeout" whenever he suspends play.

For scrimmage plays the referee's normal position is behind the scrimmage line of the team on offense.

Umpire

The umpire has primary jurisdiction over the equipment and conduct of the players.

In each scrimmage the umpire is particularly responsible for observing illegal line play and he must also cover open play that develops after linemen make their initial charge.

For scrimmage plays the umpire's normal position is behind the team on defense but he must adjust his position to the defensive formation and avoid interfering with the vision or movement of defensive players.

Linesman

The linesman has primary jurisdiction over the neutral zone and infractions of the scrimmage formation.

Under the supervision of the referee, the linesman marks the progress of the ball and keeps an accurate count of the downs. He must provide himself with assistants who remain out of bounds and conform to his directions.

Under the direction of the linesman, two assistants operate the yardage chain to mark and hold the starting point and line to gain for each series of downs.

A third assistant operates the down indicator and marks and holds the yard line through the ball's most forward point at the beginning of each down. For a scrimmage formation the linesman's normal position is in the neutral zone on one side of the field well clear of all players.

Field Judge, Back Judge, Side Judge and Line Judge

One judge has primary jurisdiction over the timing of the game, including the 25-second count. He must provide himself with a whistle and act for the referee on downfield play. The referee shall time the 25-second count with five or less officials.

The judge must start and stop the game clock as prescribed by the rules and keep the referee informed with respect to the time remaining in each period. If a foul is declared while the ball is in play, the judge shall stop the clock when the ball becomes dead.

The judge must provide himself with a stop watch and be prepared to time the game with that watch or by an assistant under his direction.

Whenever a scoreboard clock is used, the judge must observe it closely and be ready to take up timing with his stop watch if for any reason the scoreboard clock fails to function properly.

Each judge must be particularly alert to cover and rules on downfield play.

For a scrimmage, the position of the one judge is on the side of the field opposite the linesman. The positions of the other judges may be beyond the neutral zone and downfield.

British American Football Teams

NATIONAL DIVISION

Glasgow Lions
Manchester Allstars
Manchester Spartans
Nottingham Hoods
Leicester Panthers
Birmingham Bulls

Cambridge County Cats
Chelmsford Cherokees
Luton Fliers
Slough Sliverbacks
Streatham Olympians
London Ravens

Cardiff Tigers
Southampton Seahawks
Swindon Steelers
Thames Valley Chargers
Northampton Stormbringers
Milton Keynes Bucks

PREMIER DIVISION

Glasgow Diamonds
Musselburgh Magnums
Strathclyde Sheriffs
Edinburgh Blue Eagles
Tyneside Trojans
Newcastle Senators

Manchester Heroes
Scunthorpe Steelers
Steel City Giants
Leeds Cougars
Fylde Falcons
Crewe Railroaders

Wrekin Giants
Coventry Bears
Rockingham Rebels
Dunstable Cowboys
Reading Renegades
Oxford Bulldogs

Whitney Wildcats
Cotswold Bears
Hereford Chargers
Taunton Wyverns
Torbay Trojans
Plymouth Admirals

Bournemouth Bobcats
Greenwich Rams
Portsmouth Warriors
Brighton B52s
Southern Bengals

Windsor Monarchs
City of London Stags
Colchester Gladiators
Lee Valley Warriors
Heathrow Jets
London Capitals

DIVISION ONE

Johnstone Crusaders
East Kilbride Pirates
Clydesdale Colts
Ayr Burners

Washington Presidents
Leeds Cobras
Lancashire Chieftains
Bradford Dolphins

Wirral Wolves
Halton Demons
Lancashire Centurians
Stockport Falcons

Stoke Spitfires
Locomotive Derby
Black Country Nailers
Wolverhampton Outlaws

Walsall Titans
West Bromwich Fireballs
Birmingham Huskies
Swansea Dragons

Duchy Destroyers
Mounts Bay Buccaneers
Newton GWs
Western Stars

Wight Rhinos
South Star Scorpions
South Coast Sharks
Hampshire Cavaliers

Eastbourne Crusaders
Ashford Cruiser
Thanet Vikings
Medway Mustangs

Kings Lynn Patriots
Norwich Devils
Newmarket Hornets
North Herts Raiders

Southend Sabres
Basildon Braves
Thames Barriers
Grays Saxons
Chingford Centurions
Collier Row Oilers

Ealing Eagles
London Lasers
Fulham Cardinals
Ilford Blackhawks
Farnham Knights
Merton Admirals

NON-LEAGUE TEAMS (DECEMBER 1986)

Dundee Whalers
Granite City Oilers
Fife 49ers
Lothian Chieftains
Durham Saints
Hartlepool Steelers
Harrogate Hawks
Preston Pirates
West Houghton Greyhounds
Oldham Pirates
Chester Romans
Merseyside Centurions
Burton Barons
Rotherham Redskins
Boston Blitz
Lincoln Bombers
Redditch Arrows
Cheltenham Chieftains
Bridge End Colts
Cardiff AFC
Exeter Eagles

Bristol Blackhawks
Bath Gladiators
Yeovil Harriers
Britannia Royals
Gosport Vikings
Selsey Badgers
Runnymede Generals
Tonbridge Tigers
Orpington Owls
East Kent Cougars
Bexley Barons
Hinkley Hurricanes
St Albans Kestels
Leicester Panthers 2s
Brent Bandits
Wandsworth Rams
Wycombe Cheetahs
London Barbarians
Greenwich Rams 2s
Bristol Packers

Index to Rules

93

INDEX TO RULES